CARNY SIDESHOWS

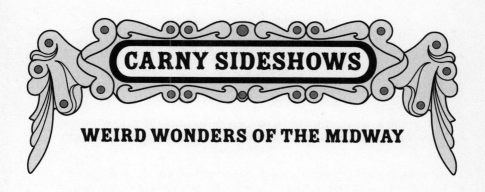

CARNY SIDESHOWS

WEIRD WONDERS OF THE MIDWAY

Tony Gangi

CITADEL PRESS BOOKS are published by

Kensington Publishing Corp.
119 West 40th Street
New York, NY 10018

All Kensington titles, imprints, and distributed lines are available at special quantity discounts for bulk purchases for sales promotions, premiums, fund-raising, educational, or institutional use. Special book excerpts or customized printings can also be created to fit specific needs. For details, write or phone the office of the Kensington special sales manager: Kensington Publishing Corp., 119 West 40th Street, New York, NY 10018, attn: Special Sales Department; phone 1-800-221-2647.

CITADEL PRESS and the Citadel logo are Reg. U.S. Pat. & TM Off.

First printing: March 2010

10 9 8 7 6 5 4 3 2 1

Printed in the United States of America

Library of Congress Control Number: 2009937072

ISBN-13: 978-0-8065-3134-2
ISBM-10: 0-8065-3134-7

For
Suzanne Elaine
who, in loving me, allows me to do what I do.
My love, what have I done to deserve you?

and

Shaffer Mycroft Nightshade
who never ceases to make me smile.
If you read between the lines, herein lies a lesson:
live life to its fullest.

CONTENTS

WARNING

This book is *not*, in any way, shape, or form, intended to be an instruction manual.

While it outlines many of the skills taught at Sideshow School, relates the experiences learning those skills, and delves into the science and anatomy that makes much of these feats possible, none of what is found within these pages is meant to be either instruction or direction.

Everything outlined herein is dangerous and should only be attempted under the tutelage of a trained and professional mentor. This book cannot, should not, and is not meant to serve as that mentor. While the science and anatomy of such feats are described in detail, the *hows are not*. Neither the author, publisher, nor anyone involved assumes any responsibility or liability or both for anyone stupid enough to try these stunts on their own.

ACKNOWLEDGMENTS

Few books are written alone, and this is no exception. First and foremost, many, many thanks go to Todd Robbins, the unnamed instructor found among these pages. I count myself lucky to have participated in one of the final few Sideshow School classes he taught at Coney Island USA. He provided hours of advice, counsel, support, and ripping yarns.

Thanks to Dick Zigun and all the folks at Coney Island USA who were kind enough to open their doors to me long after my Sideshow School experience had ended. You couldn't find a better group of performers or a better group of people more passionate about what they do. If you're truly interested in learning some of the skills found in this book, then the Coney Island Sideshow School is the place to go.

I appreciate Penn Jillette not only for sharing the great stories about Teller and himself in the early days and the way in which he became enamored of the sideshow but also for revealing his thoughts about the grind and American individualism. Thanks, also, to Glenn Alai and Laura Foley for helping make that interview happen.

Harley Newman and his unique way of looking at the world became infectious, and I thank him for that and for the time, support, and knowledge he lent to these pages.

Thanks to James Taylor, who was there long before me. He turned what I thought would be a fifteen-minute interview into an hour and a half, and he happily shared his thoughts, feelings, and experiences regarding the sideshow.

To Ward Hall, Chris M. Christ, and, of course, Pete Terhurne (Poobah) for a day I'll not soon forget. Your tales, hospitality, and memories alone were worth the trip, and for all of that I thank you. If anyone has the chance to see their *World of Wonders*, they should run, not walk, to the nearest ticket booth.

Thanks to Daryl Taylor, physics professor extraordinaire, for his ability to take scientific concepts and principles and make them accessible to a Neanderthal such as myself. Also, thanks to Evan M. Goldman, Ph.D., assistant professor at the University of Philadelphia, for providing the necessary insights into human anatomy when I needed it, and to Regan Brunetti for helping me find him when the time was right.

I am grateful to Franco Kossa and all the folks at Inkin' the Valley and *Sideshow Gathering* not only for giving their support, interest, and enthusiasm in this project but for continuing to keep the sideshow tradition alive.

Thanks to Fantasma Magic of New York City and the Palace of Wonders in Washington, DC, for their hospitality. When in New York or DC, check them out!

Much appreciation goes to Wayne N. Keyser, who was kind enough to allow me to reprint a portion of his amazing lexicon of carnival and sideshow lingo. Be sure to find him and all the fantastic carnival and sideshow information he harbors on the web at www.goodmagic.com.

To Alfie Goodrich, who, despite being half a world away, was kind enough to work with me on a photo that I fell in love with and to give me the necessary permission to use it herein along with the bit of history he had on it.

Much appeciation to Samantha X, Jason Black, Ken Pittman, Laurent Martin, and all the folks with the *999 Eyes Freakshow*, for being who you are and doing what you do. You're keeping it alive!

Eddie and Margie Gardner of DiamondsMagic.com provided much support, and were always willing to listen even though what I sometimes had to tell them or show them made them cringe.

Many, many thanks go to my wife's colleague, Stephanie

Sarokin, who not only lent the flexibility to my wife's work schedule to make my initial jaunt to Sideshow School possible but also provided an unending supply of support and love to the Gangi family, far away though we may be.

In writing this book, I stayed in many hotels and motels, some of which were seedier and more decrepit than I expected. I quickly learned that a bed, a place to rest your head, and some friendship are always good to have when you're traveling up and down the East Coast. So to the LaSusa Family—Kim, Tom, Matt, and Aidan—who were always there with their door open, thank you!

If it weren't for Rob Trimarco's hospitality—and the ever-popular RobCon—I never would have found out that while everyone can do it, not everyone wants to. Thanks, Rob!

To Grett McBean, a constant friend who appears and disappears throughout my life like the Shadow. You came through when no one else could, and I thank you for that.

Thanks to my good friends Gina Lockwood-Sheehan, Michelle Romano, and Paula Morin for their constant and undying support.

Special thanks to all of my family for their unending interest, support, love: Deb and Ed Riesch, Valerie McGuire, and Albert and Barbara Belmonte.

Heaping spoonfuls of thanks and love to my mother, Dorothy Gangi, who made the right phone call at the right time and said all the right things that made me sure I was headed in the right direction.

Thanks to the brilliant mind of Gary Goldstein (Did I say "brilliant" and that name in the same sentence? Yes I did.), good friend and editor, that this book even exists. It was Gary's offhand comment that sparked the initial concept, and it was his keen insight and constant support and encouragement that made what you have in your hands better than it was. Truly, thanks to everyone at Kensington for believing and supporting this endeavor. Selling a book about folks who hammer nails into their heads isn't an easy task, and they were able to see the potential in it.

To Jake Elwell and all the other folks at the Harold Ober Agency, I am so grateful. Jake stepped in when he did to take on a project that was a little more freaky than most—literally—and for that I thank him.

There are, quite literally, thousands of sideshow performers in the world. Regretfully, I could not meet and speak with all of them. Thanks to all the performers and lovers of the sideshow who gave of their time to either meet with me or allow me to photograph them for this book including Scott Baker, Jason Black, Damien Blade, Danny Borneo, Reggie Bügmüncher, Sally the Cinch, Crispy, Mr. Eon, Flora and Fauna, Sylver Fyre, Tyler Fyre (they're not related and they don't work together, go figure), Heather Holiday, Thrill Kill Jill, Martin Ling the Suicide King, Brett Loudermilk, The Great Nippullini, The Professor, Adam Rinn, Jonathan Royer, Roderick Russell, Sensoriel, Serpentina, Casey M. Severn, Trinket, Gwyd the Unusual, Mike Vitka, Natasha Veruschka, Donny Vomit, Doc Wilson, and Swami Yomahmi.

Finally, thanks to my wife, Suzanne, for being there after every trip home and after every interview—good and bad—you made the tough parts easy and the good parts more enjoyable. And to my son, Shaffer, hugs and thanks for always being there to make me smile.

AUTHOR'S NOTE #1

Something needs to be established from the outset. I love the sideshow.

But I'm not a sideshow man.

I love all the trappings of the *traditional* sideshow. I love the acts, from the sword-swallower to the blade box routine to the guy who collects the money for a peek inside the box to see how the girl fits in there with all those blades. I love the fire-eaters and fire-breathers. They are human dragons in the way that many of them spit out balls of fire so high and so wide that the audience can feel the heat roiling over them from the stage.

But I'm not a sideshow man.

I love the blowoff, the final, extra act that can only be procured for a few bucks more, and I love the fact that this act is, more often than not, on the cheesier, less than stellar end of things. I love the structure, the way the whole thing is put together. I love the banner line and the amazing art that goes into it, vivid colors and amazing pictures that put most advertising campaigns to shame, often exaggerating what will be seen inside the tent you're about to enter, but enduring and endearing nonetheless. I love the outside talkers and the way they almost entrap the audience, guiding them to the ticket taker with all the charm and skill of a Pied Piper.

But I'm not a sideshow man.

I paid money and sought out mentors to teach me the skills that are performed at the sideshow. I worked hard at these, honing them until I knew the safest way to present them. And

I worked hard on those presentations, because one of the things I've learned along the way is that presentation is everything. It's not enough just to do something, you have to make the good great. You have to be *entertaining*.

But I'm not a sideshow man.

I have a T-shirt that says FREAKSHOW, CONEY ISLAND, USA. One of my e-mail addresses has the word sideshow woven into it (I have too many e-mail addresses, but that's a different subject altogether). I have numerous books in my library about the sideshow, about the history of this unusual institution, and about the way in which it has grown over the years and the many ways it has changed and evolved.

But I'm not a sideshow man.

I've had friends and I've learned that friends come and go. They step into your life for a time, then seem to disappear. Some are memorable, others not so much. But some of the best, most enjoyable times I've had and some of the most interesting and provocative conversations I've been engaged in have been with the people you'll find in these pages.

But no matter what, I'm not a sideshow man.

I'm an outsider. It's as simple as that. I'm an outsider with a love for the sideshow, and while I may have learned the skills and talked to all the right people and done all my research, I'm still an outsider. I may love the sideshow, but I'm not a sideshow man.

All this needs to be established at the outset because I don't want to present myself as something I'm not. I'm not "with it," as the carnies would say, indicating someone on the inside or "in the know." I'm an outsider who was given the opportunity and privilege to peel back the canvas flap and play inside for a bit. That's all.

Ward Hall, one of the finest and most authentic sideshow men I've met, put it best:

> There are many people who claim they are sideshow men. But in my opinion a sideshow man is the guy who

has sat up all night with the fat girl in the hospital, who has held the crying midget woman who has just lost her midget husband who died, or when you have to change the tire in the rain on a muddy road for the armless girl. That's when you're a sideshow man.

That being said, allow me to reiterate, no, I'm not a sideshow man—but I love the sideshow.

AUTHOR'S NOTE #2

Coney Island USA offers two opportunities every spring and fall to attend Sideshow School. To the best of my knowledge, the same material is taught in each section, but these sections are offered in two different ways depending on your availability. The first is a typical Monday through Friday format, with classes running anywhere from 11 A.M. to 5 P.M. The second offers those with day jobs a chance to take the course with classes being offered on a weekday evening five consecutive weeks in a row. When I attended Sideshow School, I opted for the Monday through Friday format. The schedule was easier for me.

However, it should be noted that during the course of that week the stunts learned at Sideshow School were taught in a fashion that allowed the skills to be built on so that certain goals were achieved. For example, we learned how to make a torch before we learned how to extinguish it in our mouths, and we learned to extinguish it long before we learned to spit or breathe it. Some skills are needed to be learned before others in much the same way you need to learn to add, subtract, multiply, and divide long before you make any attempts at algebra.

For simplicity's sake, I've tinkered with, and taken certain liberties with, this schedule. While I've chronicled my time at Sideshow School here as learning a skill a day, this was not the case. Certain skills and stunts need to be built on, and nothing as dangerous as sideshow skills can or should be learned in a day.

In the "Sideshow Mentors, Performers, and Resources" chapter (195), you'll find the listings for numerous sideshow performers, some of whom also teach sideshow skills. If you're interested in learning these strange feats, I suggest you seek one of them out, such as Harley Newman, or contact Coney Island USA about their next series of classes. Pertinent contact information can be found in this chapter.

INTRODUCTION

*It seems to me that people have vast potential.
Most people can do extraordinary things if they
have the confidence or take the risks. Yet most
people don't.*

—Philip Adams

*Today's show promises to be a marvelous cele-
bration of the human spirit.*

—Sideshow Bob, *The Simpsons*

Enjoy every sandwich.   —Warren Zevon

At one time, the boards of the stage at the *Coney Island Circus
Sideshow* were painted a bright red. Now they were dull, dusty,
and cracked, as was the slender banister that ran around the
perimeter of the stage area. Or maybe it was just the dim lighting or a trick memory that nostalgia plays. I'm still not sure.

Six of us were gathered around that banister eyeing the three
items the instructor had set before us: a nail, a Phillips head

screwdriver, and an ice pick. The nail and screwdriver, I estimated, were approximately four inches long, the ice pick a bit longer. Of the three items, it was my summation that the ice pick could be problematic for a number of reasons:

First, the tip was incredibly sharp. So much so that if it was flung to the floor at just the right angle—as our instructor had done—it would penetrate the wood and stand upright. Of course, an amateur, such as myself, could feasibly miss the floor and hit his foot. Such catastrophes are best saved for private moments when no one else is around. Fortunately, my limp was undetectable for the remainder of the day. Note to self: purchase steel-toed shoes.

Second, the length of the ice pick seemed to be more than four inches. It seemed closer to six—maybe six and a half inches—whereas the depth of my head can be measured at around six inches or so. Every instinct I had was telling me that the math on the ice pick wasn't exactly in my favor.

The keen-eyed and quick-witted thinkers should be asking themselves at this point what the depth of my head had to do with anything at all. This being Sideshow School, the depth of my head was exceedingly important since we were attempting something known as the Human Blockhead.* In brief, the Human Blockhead is a sideshow act that involves the hammering of a nail or the insertion of some other item into the nose. Usually the item can be inserted fairly deep, but if something were inserted too far, then you risk hitting the back of your head where a little something called the medulla oblongata rests. This is better known as the brain stem, and best respected at all costs.

The risks were clear, and there we stood. Our instructor had asked us to choose one of the items and insert it into our respective nasal passages. I wasn't sure but could probably guess that this *wasn't* the approved use for any of these items. I

---

* Please see glossary for definitions of carnival and sideshow terms and lingo.

glanced at the choices one more time, hoping they'd changed into something a bit more nasal-friendly. It would've been nice to have at least one option that might not, should I make a monumental mistake—as I'd done earlier with the ice pick in estimating where my foot ended and the floor began—cause any internal bleeding or, god forbid, brain damage. My wife would have contested that I must have had some form of brain damage even to consider attending Sideshow School in the first place.

"Choose one of the items and gently probe around a bit; then once you find the passage we've been exploring, insert the item into that passage."

I took in the items one last time. Nope, they still hadn't changed. The old *Sesame Street* skit played through my head: one of these things is not like the others. If that axiom were true, then I'd be damned if I could figure out what the right choice was. But then again, I couldn't imagine Big Bird, Ernie, Bert, or Kermit, hell, I couldn't even imagine Oscar the Grouch, inserting any of those items into his head, and he lived in a garbage can—and was made of foam.

"Your turn."

All eyes were on me. When you're in Sideshow School, some-one's always the center of attention. Sometimes, even though you've chosen to be there, you don't want it to be you. I'd had jobs in the past, office jobs, where I'd be at a meeting and it was my turn to speak, my turn to add to the group and throw my thoughts into the mix. Or it would be my turn to aid in a brainstorming session to inform my superiors and col-leagues exactly what I was bringing to the table to earn my weekly paycheck. And in retrospect, each of those moments paled in comparison to moments in the spotlight at Sideshow School.

With a tentative hand I reached out and took the nail. We were provided with alcohol swabs so that we could clean the item before inserting it. I understand that they also swab the arm of death row inmates before executing them. Just a thought.

I tilted my head back and hoped that what I'd heard was true: there was no real danger of brain damage since the copious amounts of blood squirting out would be warning enough that I'd gone too far. Gently I inserted the nail into my nostril. It entered, then went deeper, and deeper, and deeper.

Sideshow School. What had I gotten myself into? And an even more curious question: Why? I could probably narrow down the answer or answers, as the case may be.

Growing up I had a strong proclivity for, and love of, magic. Magicians, misdirection, deception, all of it fascinated me to no end, as did the relationship between the magician and audience. Here you had a performer who sought to deceive and lie to the spectators, and the spectators were ready, willing, and able to be deceived. And, in addition, the magician, utilizing basic methods of misdirection also employed rudimentary psychology in order to achieve the miracles that the audience believed they were witnessing. It was, indeed, a strange relationship.

Most of my young adult life I pursued magic as a hobby, and as an adult, I pursued it even more vigorously as I attempted to gain meaningful employment performing and attempting to turn my hobby into an actual paying job. Life was good. I enjoyed what I was doing.

Except for one thing, one memory that seemed to linger at the very outer reaches of my subconscious. Even today, I have only a few pieces of the memory at best, but the pieces are clear ones, easily recognizable, and even easier to interpret. Most importantly, there are enough pieces of this memory to assemble a recognizable picture.

I must have been anywhere between the ages of six and eight years old. My parents decided to take me to the circus. Now, this wasn't one of the big names. It wasn't Ringling or the Big Apple or even Cole Bros. To the best of my knowledge it wasn't. This was sometime during the 1970s in suburban Pennsylvania. It was in either the spring or the fall, when carnivals, fairs, circuses, and the like, would spring up in empty parking lots and unused fields almost overnight, as if out of a Ray Bradbury novel.

This one, the name of which still eludes me to this day, was erected in the far corner of a mall parking lot. There were two tents, one larger and brightly colored, the other smaller with a white, garish canvas covered in tears, holes, and patches. Outside the smaller tent's entrance stood a stage, and on that stage stood two men, one bellowing into a microphone, the other standing placidly nearby with a handful of razor blades and paper. My parents and I stood at the base of the stage as the crowd filled in around us. As the "outside talker" (a term I later learned referred to the man ranting on the stage, sometimes also called a "barker") ran through his spiel, the other man began to shred a sheet of paper with one of the razor blades, then he stuck out his tongue, placed a blade on his tongue, and proceeded to eat the razor blades.

I stood by my father's side, slack jawed and stunned. One after another the razor blades went into the man's mouth. He chewed them, and we were close enough to the stage so that you could audibly hear the blades pop in his mouth as his teeth ground down on them. Finally, after popping some ten blades into his mouth, he spat the broken metal shards out into a bowl for all to see, then opened his mouth, peeling his checks apart and sticking out his tongue as proof that he remained unharmed. My father led us away.

Though I wanted to see what was inside the smaller tent, my parents didn't deem it appropriate fare for a child my age, so it was to the circus we went. As I was dragged from the smaller tent, I got a glimpse inside. The flap was pulled back, and there I could clearly make out a tiny crowd gathered on bleachers. They watched as a man, lying on a bed of nails, held a cinder block on his chest. Another man stood over him with a sledgehammer and brought the full weight of the tool down onto the stone block. The gasp of the crowd and the crack of the cinder block are the final memories I have of what was my first sideshow.

What is a sideshow? In its essence, in its heart, the sideshow is a collection of misfits celebrating their uniqueness. As Todd Robbins, author and sideshow performer, pointed out to me, "One of the appeals of the freak act is that everyone has a touch of the freak about them. Everyone has something about them that they're a little bit ashamed of, that sets them apart in their eyes in a *not good* way. And the sideshow says, 'Don't hide it, celebrate it.'"

The sideshow is the place where such things can be celebrated. And more and more, it's not only their uniqueness these folks are celebrating but their unparalleled ability to push their bodies to the very reaches of what they can do. They stand determined to show their audiences and the world that there is more to life and that there is more that they can do with these shells they call bodies. There is untapped potential lying in wait for each man and each woman, and they're here to prove it. They're living, breathing proof that there's more to life than the daily grind of the office cubicle and the watercooler. They're here to show us and, at times, shock us into the reality of the world.

Sideshow performers are people who are truly alive on the inside, and they want you to be too. After all, we're all misfits to one degree or another, born of a country of misfits. Our forefathers came to this country seeking a home, turning their backs on lands, kingdoms, and sovereignties that deemed their religious, personal, or political beliefs contrary to the norm.

They were misfits. And the sideshow is the place where misfits can celebrate being themselves and where one's uniqueness and one's rare and special individuality can thrive for all to see. What could be more American than that?

Now before anyone goes hammering nails into their noses while reciting the Pledge of Allegiance with the "Star-Spangled Banner" echoing in the background, there are some facts that need to be set straight. America didn't *invent* the sideshow.

Many people, wrongly, believe that it was P. T. Barnum who invented the sideshow, but this is not necessarily true. "It's a Barnum sort of exercise, now that I think about it," noted James Taylor, author and publisher of *Shocked and Amazed: On & Off the Midway*. "Because Barnum didn't invent 99% of the things people think he invented. At all. He didn't invent the circus, he didn't invent the sideshow, he didn't invent the dime museum. But he *perfected* them. He *did* invent modern advertising, and there are those that would argue, and I'd be one of them, that he invented modern New York."

Before acts such as sword-swallowing, fire-eating, and the Human Blockhead found their ways into the capable hands of P. T. Barnum and the sideshow, they existed throughout the world in various forms performed by a variety of peoples. Middle Eastern priests and Indian fakirs used such feats regularly as ways to not only draw crowds but prove that the gods had blessed them. Oh, and they were also able to sell a few things after the sermon, as well, but that's neither here nor there. Is it?

"American sideshows, the '10-in-1' tradition, are not *unknown* elsewhere," Taylor said. "Sideshows are not *unknown* elsewhere, but it's the way America honed the tradition, and the way Americans just seem to become identified as the sideshow nation. It is really the metaphor for the twenty-first century.

"They've had sideshows in Japan, they've had sideshows in Central America, South America, Africa's got sideshows, they come from different places and different traditions except that they're all driven by human curiosity and the need to have things learned by having things presented to you. It's the *show* business is what it is."

These oddly bizarre acts were utilized by performers throughout the world for a variety of reasons—and for centuries—before finding their ways to the shores of America, eventually being gathered together into a single show. You might say that the Industrial Revolution had a lot to do with it.

It was in the late eighteenth century and early part of the nineteenth century that the Industrial Revolution began seriously to influence America as a nation. The scales started to tip in America to that of an industrial nation from that of an agrarian.

Industrial? Agrarian? What does all this mean, and what in the world does it have to do with the sideshow? These words should be confined to the classroom and shouldn't enter into even the most cursory discussion of glass-eaters, sword-swallowers, bug-munchers, and their ilk. Well, industrial and agrarian have a lot to do with it. A lot.

Before machines came along, turning us into the industrial beast we are today, and made our nation smaller while at the same time bigger, America was mostly agrarian. That's not to say that we were pagans on the hunt for strangers to torch and barbecue alive inside a Wicker Man once every vernal equinox to appease the gods for a fruitful harvest (thumbs up if you conjured images of Christopher Lee and Edward Woodward). Rather, it just refers to the fact that we were a nation whose driving force were the farms woven into the American landscape. Agriculture was king. The towns and cities scattered across America's heartland were collections of people who, from day to day, worked the land. These were people who grew the food that fed us and cared for the animals that provided what was needed to clothe us. And, damn, what little free time these fine folks had must have been boring as shit because by the time the circus was born these folks were ripe for the picking—which bring us to P. T. Barnum.

Barnum struck a deal with two businessmen, William Cameron Coup and Dan Costello, to create *P. T. Barnum's Grand Traveling Museum, Menagerie, Caravan, and Circus.* The show was full of over-the-top spectacle and was exactly what people had come to expect from Barnum. But it wasn't long before good ole Phineas Taylor Barnum came up with a shrewd money-making idea, something that could be added onto the circus and bring in a few extra bucks.

Next to the circus tent, he arranged another tent to be erected. This secondary tent utilized many of the acts and displays from his famous museums, the human oddities he'd become acquainted with, and other performers such as sword-swallowers and fire-eaters. Thus the sideshow as we know it was born.

So you have America, a nation that was still fiddling with a new invention called the radio and no television in sight. Once word got around that a circus or sideshow was coming to town, everything nearly came to a standstill. Maybe it wasn't that dramatic, but traveling circuses and sideshows of that latter part of the nineteenth and early part of the twentieth century thrived on riding the rails and going from town to town providing entertainment for these folks who were the backbone of America.

Then, of course, radio, television, and movies came along and things began to change, particularly with regard to how people spent their entertainment dollars and where they found that entertainment.

Carnivals soon became a big deal, and sideshows found a life among them as well. But eventually carnivals changed as well. Everything changes, and everything evolves. The same is true of the sideshow.

The traveling sideshow lived and breathed going from one

town to the next during the late nineteenth and early twentieth centuries. In America it grew, lived, died, evolved, changed, and disintegrated, and if you look in the right places, it is rising again like a fiery Phoenix. But no matter what, through it all, the sideshow has held the public's fascination, offering entertainment both unique and bizarre.

Traditionally structured to include ten acts in one, the 10-in-1, or sideshow, is composed of a multitude of performers, from human and animal oddities to magic and illusions, curios, and trained animal shows. Most acts that fall under these banners require particular and distinctive entertainers not easily found, such as Siamese twins, the grossly obese (though some might argue that these folks are more easily found in the wilds of America as opposed to other places around the world), little people, deformed animals, or the use of specially made large-scale illusions such as the classic sideshow exhibit Girl to Gorilla, where a young woman visually transforms into an ape. There is, however, one last category of sideshow entertainer that almost anyone can aspire to, the working act.

Working acts are the meat of the 10-in-1 and are composed of entertainers who have made a conscious choice to be different. Unlike those performers who are born different, performers that comprise a sideshow's working acts have gone out of their way to stand out. Through vigorous learning, practice, a bit of blood, and more than a few burns, these people have acquired and mastered a particular skill or skills. The basic working acts found in most sideshows include lying on a bed of nails, fire-eating, performing the human blockhead (hammering a nail into your nasal passage), walking on broken glass, snake charming, mastering the use of animal traps (jamming your hand or tongue into any form of animal trap without being harmed), and sword-swallowing.

Sideshows attract audiences with these acts in much the same way as car crashes: people can't help but watch, covering their eyes but peeking through their fingers nonetheless. And while we want to watch, few people would ever consider attempting the feats presented on the dusty painted boards of a sideshow stage, which is exactly how I felt, until I attended Sideshow School.

On a Monday morning in April 2007, while my friends and family dropped off their children at day care centers and went off to their respective jobs and while millions of Americans went about their lives, arriving at schools or businesses that would see their days playing out in front of a desk or confined to a cubicle, I attended Sideshow School, learning the bare basics of the working acts and the ins and outs of the sideshow.

What was it that caused me to set out on this venture? Why would anyone, in their right mind, decide one day that they desperately needed to know how to eat fire and jam various and assorted body parts into the traps of animals? What was it that convinced me I had a need to walk on broken glass and learn how to insert varied and numerous items into my nasal passage? There can be a number of answers, some such as idiocy, stupidity, and sheer recklessness. These I try to ignore when they're presented to me at the dinner table.

Most of my life I've not been idiotic, stupid, or reckless. Some might contend that I've played it entirely too safe on occasion, far from reckless. No, some of the other answers are closer to the truth.

Certainly it had something to do with my experiences as a boy, being exposed, albeit briefly, to a sideshow performer and the seemingly endless wonders that waited for me on the other side of the tent flap. It's all alive on the inside! Wonders wrapped in the canvas of a tent were being denied me by an adult. If there is anything sure to make an impression on a child, it is censorship. Ask anyone whose EC Comics were taken away from them as a child, denying them their

Vault of Horrors and *Tales from the Crypt.* Those children found a way to get their hands on them, one way or another.

It also had more than a little to do with my interest in magic, but therein lies a peculiar rub. You see, if ever there were polar opposites in the world, it is magic and the sideshow. While magic deals in lies (honest lies, true) and deception, there is, in the sideshow, veritably little deception involved in what these performers are actually doing onstage. The sideshow's tagline could almost read, "What you see is what you get."

In magic you have a cornucopia of secret moves, deceptive sleights, and hidden gaffs. In the sideshow, the only deception is the exploitation of the audience's lack of knowledge. The audience doesn't know, for example, that the human anatomy makes it not only probable but possible to hammer a nail into your nose. The sideshow exploits this knowledge and, in turn, presents something amazing. So after enmeshing myself in the conjuring arts, practicing hour after hour on card sleights and hidden moves, I found the very concept of "what you see is what you get" very refreshing.

The skills of a magician are the unsung heroes of the magic show. Never will an audience truly know the countless hours of practice that made a specific trick, illusion, or miracle possible. In the sideshow, however, the skill is there, it's real, it's tangible, it's alive, and it's in our face, in the faces of every audience member so they might witness it for themselves, some from between their fingers.

There is one final reason why I decided to attend Sideshow School. It's something a bit different from these other reasons and one that might not be that surprising, but certainly relevant to my motivations. But this last reason I think I'll save for the end, a blowoff to be revealed at the time of egress, if you want to put it in sideshow terminology.

So we're headed for Sideshow School. We'll learn a bit about the acts, we'll learn a bit about some of the amazing performers working in the sideshow today, and we'll take a brief look at the history behind the sideshow. We'll even learn a thing or two about the science of how this is done. We'll discover hammering nails and lighting torches isn't as hard as it seems. So follow me through the flap. It's all alive on the inside. But take my advice: buy yourself a pair of steel-toed shoes first.

CHAPTER ONE

〜〜

SIDESHOW SCHOOL

or, After Four Years of College, You're Doing What???

And the older boy, bless his soul, is preparing for his career.... Yeah, last season he was a pixie-dust spreader on the Tilt-O-Whirl. He thinks maybe next year he'll be guessing people's weight or barking for the Yak woman.
—Randy Quaid as Cousin Eddie,
National Lampoon's Christmas Vacation

Four years of college; two years of grad school; six years total and untold amounts of money; classroom after boring classroom, and I have to admit that while higher education did, at times, capture my interest, there had to be a way to jazz up the method with which the information was disseminated. The college I attended for both my undergraduate degree and graduate degree was one in the same, and offered nothing more than bland rooms with walls painted in an eye-popping forgettable gray, uncomfortable seats that would ultimately lead to back problems in later life, chalkboards that produced such vast amounts of dust that you risked contracting "white lung disease," and the occasional professor who spent most of the time sauntering around death's doorstep. Rather than fire extinguishers in the corners of the room, you fully expected to find defibrillators available in case one keeled over in the middle of an exam. Alternatively, should the professor be of good enough health, he invariably wore a toupee atop his head that—possibly given his pay scale—was either too large or too small. Next to the defibrillator should have been a glass-covered box with a hairpiece in it with a note on top that read, "In case of hair loss break glass."

The American educational experience has, for the most part, crossed well over the line into the land of the mundane, a place where nothing unexpected happens and where lessons are created and presented by applying the Ben Stein/*Ferris Bueller* axiom of Information + Monotone (x Boredom) = Education.

It's a relief that neither Ben Stein nor any of the professors I experienced during my college years ever swallowed a sword or ate fire. I fear that they might have injected the act with boredom hereto unknown by the sideshow community.

Which begs the question: Where does one learn such things as sideshow skills? Is it in a room filled with fire extinguishers and medical gear and a nurse waiting in the wings should something go horribly wrong? The answer, thankfully, is no.

Initially, the day I signed on for the course, I went to bed that night with certain images in my head of what the class might be like for me: a man on stage swallowing a sword, a performer blasting fire into the air, a midget on a unicycle, bare feet crunching on glass, vibrant banners surrounding scads of people hammering nails into their noses, Siamese twins talking backward and reciting the Gettysburg Address, and tongues hanging from mouths like dogs panting in the heat, mousetraps affixed to each of them. And aside from the midget and the Siamese twins, my imaginings were spot on.

Tell anyone that you're attending Sideshow School, and the mind reels with the possibilities. For the most part, what the mind comes up with is in a near dead heat to being exactly what the reality of Sideshow School is. You don't find yourself in a stifling room being fed information as a mother would spoon-feed her child, nor do you find the environment overly cautious and fearful of injury. Rather, Sideshow School is a hands-on environment where the only way to learn something is to do it. And you do it all where you would perform it all: on a stage. And the stage where I went to learn it all was on Coney Island, which I'd visited more than once before and after Sideshow School to take in their sideshow.

Donny Vomit—an ideal name for a sideshow performer if there ever was one—is standing on stage juggling. It's toward the end of the show, and it's wrapped up with a unique routine in which Vomit juggles a flaming torch, a machete, and an apple. Infused with Vomit's signature wit and humor and the crossbreeding of said humor with a visceral tension felt by the audience, the act requires Vomit not only to juggle the items but to take bites from the apple while doing so.

The audience, for its part, laughs at the jokes, enjoys the juggling, and hopes secretly for Vomit's curled moustache to catch fire, for him to lob off a finger with the machete, or to see him accidentally bite the head of the flaming torch as if it were the apple—none of which happens. But the audience applauds loudly and enthusiastically nonetheless, leaving the *Coney Island Circus Sideshow* satisfied and pleased that they'd gotten much more than their money's worth on this bright Saturday afternoon.

Much like Vomit's routine, Coney itself is facing a bit of a juggling act. All in all Coney Island is a city in flux. That's nothing new for Coney Island though. While residents and businesses continue an ongoing fight with the city and real estate developers over the future of the city and what it will become, this place, nostalgically referred to as the City of Fire after it was illuminated at the turn of the century, its twinkling lights cutting through the darkness for miles, throbs with life nonetheless.

Seated by the sea just outside of Manhattan, Coney Island was the home for some of the most spectacular amusement parks in the world. At a time when entertainment was at a premium—hey, look at the folks in middle America, the circus or sideshow or both coming to town was a big deal—Coney Island provided a respite for people living in Manhattan, Long Island, or New Jersey. In the early part of the twentieth century, it was *the* place to go, where the beaches would teem with bodies clad in bathing suits designed to show as little flesh as possible, and the boardwalk was home to places such as Dreamland, Steeplechase, and Luna Park. There might be a million tales to be told of the naked city, but for Coney Island there's probably a billion—or two billion. But now in this time of change, a new chapter is being written in the history of Coney Island, and what sort of future it brings this city has yet to be written. But, certainly, one of the places that will follow through to that future will be the organization known as Coney Island USA.

Situated in a building on the corner of 12th Street and Surf Avenue on Coney Island, Coney Island USA is a nonprofit arts organization founded by Dick Zigun, who is one of those rare, true, through-and-through lovers of bizarre American culture, which isn't surprising when you take into consideration that Zigun grew up in Bridgeport, Connecticut, the home of the original showman, P. T. Barnum himself. In his youth, Zigun attended such Bridgeport staples as the *Wingding Parade* and the *Barnum Festival* that the city hosted each summer. All of these were surely nothing more than the ingredients of a larger recipe for low-level brainwashing or, possibly, a sort of *Boys from Brazil* gone haywire, with the goal being the reintroduction of not Hitler but Barnum into twenty-first-century society. "By the time I was nine years old," Zigun said, "I was a Barnum scholar and convinced elephants and midgets were patriotic."

Making just as deep an impression on Zigun as the city in

which he spent his youth was the first sideshow he witnessed, at which he had the opportunity to see the *John Strong Sideshow*. It was there that he and his family watched Melvin Burkhart, the man who made the Human Blockhead act famous in America, hammer a nail that appeared to be the size of a railroad spike into his head.

"We would go down to Seaside Park where the Straight Show would come in. And my dad was a big fan of being cheap and having us walk around and watch the Veg-O-Matic guy for free. Now, even at an early age I was always advocating to go into the sideshow. And one year my father decided we were all old enough. I have a brother that's three years older and twin sisters that are five years younger. So we all went into the sideshow. My sister Renee watched Melvin Burkhart hammer a nail into his head, and vomited. And somehow my career choice was decided then and there," Zigun said.

You can't get family entertainment any better than that, can you? That experience sealed Zigun's fate. He attained two degrees in theater, one of which was an MFA from the Yale School of Drama, and then moved to New York City. But instead of aspiring to the Great White Way, he turned his attention to Coney Island.

"I was crazy and knew that Coney Island was *the* place to use as a staging ground," he said. "Because here it's not art *about* popular culture, it *is* popular culture."

Coney Island USA runs their sideshow seasonally, from April until mid to late September. The shows operate most weekdays and every weekend, with performers hitting the stage at one in the afternoon. The run time of the show is approximately a half an hour, and once one show ends the next begins almost immediately (this is called a grind), thus, it's constantly running throughout the day. Showing up in the middle of one show? That's fine. Stay until you've seen what you've already seen, and then find your way to the egress (that's exit to you and me). "We're doing the same grind they were doing a hundred years ago," Zigun noted.

The only difference being that Coney Island USA's show isn't a traveling sideshow. It's stationary. The downside of which is that unless you're visiting New York City, no one else in the country has the opportunity to see exactly how good this show is.

The *Coney Island Circus Sideshow* operates on the 10-in-1 structure, that is, you're seeing ten acts in one show. Not all sideshows operate on this structure. Some might have a handful of acts (4 or 5) as well as a small museum of curios or other bizarre objects or might have living animal oddities such as a two-headed calf or snake. A few years back I attended a Strawberry Festival on Long Island and stumbled on something sideshow folks like to call a single-o, a single act or sideshow exhibit housed in a lone tent. On this occasion the tent claimed to harbor a giant horse. "HUMONGOUS!" and "GARGANTUAN!" the tent banners read. After paying our few bucks, my friend, Tom LaSusa, and I entered to find a Clydesdale. It's all in your perspective. In comparison to other horses, the Clydesdale surely *is* a giant horse. And that's how sideshows work. Sometimes they're really showing you that two-headed snake or calf they're claiming to have, and sometimes the truth is bent as far as it can be bent before it entirely snaps off.

So the structure of the sideshow is flexible. Don't have enough acts? Then make one up. Or find another act. Back in 1997 or 1998 when I first stumbled on the *Coney Island Circus Sideshow*, one of the acts was an insect eater, a woman who hunkered down before the audience and gobbled fistfuls of maggots and other creepy crawlies. While that act isn't in the Coney Island show's current incarnation, they've found other acts to include to keep the audiences paying to get in. There's *always* something people will pay to see.

The *Coney Island Circus Sideshow* runs on ten solid acts woven into an incredibly tight-knit show. Though it must be said that it does suffer at times from the grind. While it's certainly honorable that they're doing a constant grind similar to what sideshows did years ago, it does at times visibly wear on the performers. I had the opportunity to see the sixth or seventh show into the grind on one day, and the first show of the grind on another day. The energy level was markedly different, which when you consider how many shows they're doing, isn't unexpected. And that's not to say the show where the energy level was down wasn't a good one. For me seeing a sideshow has gotten to be a bit like sex, pizza, or hamburgers. Even the bad ones are good ones.

I've seen the *Coney Island Circus Sideshow* many times over the years since first seeing it, and each year the lineup of acts changes slightly. This year the acts included the human blockhead, snake charming, sword-swallowing, the blade box (an illusion), a freak act (a true human oddity), Miss Electro (an act using electricity coursing through a performer's body), a brief trap act, juggling, a whip act, and a fire act, giving us ten acts.

An offbeat thought hits me partway through the show that this strange sort of menagerie of entertainers that Coney Island USA features had all at one time or another sought to attend some form of sideshow school. Maybe it wasn't anything nearly as organized as the Sideshow School that Coney Island USA offers today, but at one time they searched for a mentor to teach them what they now feature to curious onlookers on a daily basis. They made a conscious choice not only to learn these skills but to set themselves apart from others, to make themselves different, and to feature their differences in the spotlight.

Collect these performers in one place, and what you have is a menagerie: Donny Vomit, juggler and human blockhead; Heather Holiday, sword-swallower and blade box contortionist; Serpentina, snake charmer and electric chair performer; and Jason Black, a true anatomical wonder or freak. It reads like the casting call for a B movie, but makes for the pieces of a show that can keep any audience rapt with attention.

Donny Vomit hails from Oklahoma and has the appearance of an old Western saloon piano player, his well-groomed, curled and twisted moustache underscoring his wry smile and the glint in his eyes. His love of the sideshow and desire to be in one brought him to Coney Island.

"Around 1997, I joined my first sideshow," Vomit recalled. *"Rouks Circus Pandemonium.* A glorious name for what was a handful of teenage friends looking to do anything different. We were living in the middle of the Bible Belt in Oklahoma and wanting to shock and amaze anyone we could. The troupe itself burnt fast and bright (sometimes literally) and only performed a handful of shows. Performers tired of the stunts or moved on to bands, or girlfriends, or school. I stuck with it.

"I continued to perform solo throughout my college years. Punk and Rockabilly shows are where I cut my teeth. Once I hit my midtwenties, I had to make a hard choice, stay in Oklahoma with my friends and family or move to the only place that I could think of to make a living hammering nails into my face. I went to Coney Island."

Within a few months of moving to New York, Vomit landed the job of talker on the bally stage at the *Coney Island Circus Sideshow*, where he performed (and still performs) three acts per show, eight shows per day, five days a week, six months a year. This was his dream job.

In the show, Vomit acts as a sort of narrator or host, as well as performing a human blockhead routine where he not only hammers a nail into his nose but also uses a power drill to drive a spinning bit into his head. He also recites a nasty little poem about the relationship between his tongue and a mousetrap, and does the edge-of-your-seat juggling routine mentioned earlier.

As the group's snake charmer, Serpentina dances and mesmerizes one of the largest and longest albino pythons you've ever seen. Heaving the snake over her shoulders, she towers over the audience as she moves about the stage, undulating and dancing, all the while keeping constant control of the snake and attempting to convey to the audience that, through it all, through the dance and this very different kind of grind, she and the snake are almost one. There's real danger here, as other snake charmers have been bitten quite badly. Not venomous, python bites are still powerful and can draw blood. And a rule of thumb is never to be alone with one since pythons kill their prey through suffocation via constriction. And true to her art, once the 2008 season ended, she found her way to a surgeon who split her tongue in a manner befitting a snake charmer. Her forked tongue now adds to her appeal as a snake charmer.

And despite Heather Holiday's diminutive frame, she works as the troupe's sword-swallower (gentlemen in the back row, please keep your innuendo-laced comments to yourselves, thank you very much). Using her size to her advantage, Holiday shocks the audience with her skill and leaves them wondering how she can get swords the lengths of the ones she's using down her throat.

"When I perform a show, sure, I kind of want people to get grossed out," Holiday said. "But more than anything, I want to prove them wrong about whatever they assume can't be done."

Holiday also performs the Blade Box routine. A staple of sideshows for many years, the blade box is an illusion where either an illusionist or assistant crawls into a box similar to a coffin and fourteen or more blades (most running the width of six to twelve inches) are then thrust into the top of the box. Their tips are extended and visibly seen protruding from the bottom of the box. This forces the person within to contort his or her body around the blades for survival.

If this were presented by the likes of David Copperfield, the woman would enter the box, the blades would be inserted, the woman's hand would appear to show that she was safe, Copperfield would do his dance (so very similar to the old Richard Simmons workout videos, but that's neither here nor there), the blades would be removed, and the woman would exit the box unharmed. But this isn't a magic show, this is the sideshow.

Things are done differently here. And, yes, the performer does still enter the box and exit the box unharmed. It's what happens in between that's different. Probably, this act would give David Copperfield an aneurism or some kind of fit.

Once Holiday is inside the box and the blades are inserted, the audience is then invited to come up onto the stage and look down into the box to see exactly how her body is contorted around the blades. The secret to the illusion is revealed for all to see—for a price of course. Usually some small sum is asked from the audience, giving the sideshow a few more dollars income.

The way the routine is structured and scripted traditionally relates a tale of woe regarding the performer in the box, detailing how she gets no money from performing in the sideshow, but any money "donated" to see her contorted figure within the blade box will go directly to her and her starving family. Pulls at the heartstrings, doesn't it? Even if it didn't, curiosity more often than not gets the best of most people, and they are more than willing to fork over another dollar to see this mystery of the ages. Then there's the Freak Act.

In 2007, while I attended Sideshow School, word came in that they'd hired Chuy the Wolfboy from Spain. A genuine genetic anomaly, Chuy inherited a condition that caused hair to grow over every inch of his body, from head to toe.

The summer of 2008, Coney Island was lucky to have with them Jason Black of Austin, Texas. Black describes himself as "a natural-born freak show performer known as the Black

Scorpion, who uses illusions to illustrate life as a human oddity." Black Scorpion is the name he uses when performing.

Jason's birth condition is known as Ectrodactyly, which is
the medical term for the fact that his fingers were fused together prior to birth. For Jason this is true of both hands, but
this is not always the case for people exhibiting Ectrodactyly,
with some exhibiting it in only one hand.

Now with the Freak acts, many people labor under the incorrect assumption that it relies and thrives on the exploitation of the performer's "disability" or whatever makes that
person unique—which is not the case. Rather, it is truly a cel-
ebration of that person's uniqueness and an opportunity to
learn what life is like given that person's condition, what it
was like growing up, what that person does to deal with everyday situations, and so on.

"Growing up is different for everyone I'd guess," Jason said,
"I took (what I call) the Chris Farley approach—make fun of
yourself before others could and do it better than they ever
could and in doing that you can usually make fun of others
as well without getting into too much trouble."

Black takes the stage in what seems to be a hailstorm of
self-deprecation and humor that quickly catches the audience
by surprise, disarming them and allowing him the opportunity not only to explain what it's like to live with hands such
as his (it's damn hard to learn to tie your shoes for one thing,
and he shows us how he does it), but to turn the tables on,
and poke fun at, folks who have five fingers on each hand.

"My intentions are nothing but positive, to change the
hearts and minds of the five-fingered world in which we live,"
Black said.

His presentation smacks of humor and throbs with information, and any sense that this is exploitative or that Jason
suffers from a "disability" dissipates the longer you watch him.
I'm caught off guard when I ask Black one of my stock sideshow

performer questions: What won't you do and why? And the response I get back is, "Sign language, it's too complicated."

"I like audiences to walk away having laughed and been amazed. I want people to learn that being born different does not make one less of a person or performer. I'd like to be an inspiration for those born different, I want them to see that they can do whatever their hearts desire."

The sideshow experience is complete and topped off with Scott Baker as the outside talker, drawing the crowds into the show. And, in addition, the building is decorated with artwork and banners painted by Marie Roberts, stunning salutes to the sideshow banners of yesteryear. There are banners for the various acts, and one that, years earlier, caught my attention: Sideshow School.

It was in this circus-like atmosphere that Sideshow School was created. The classes take place here during the course of the year and are taught right on the stage where the performers ply their trades seasonally.

Along with Donny Vomit, the other current instructor at Sideshow School is Adam Rinn. While they weren't the instructors at my session of the course, they now handle the daily duties of teaching this class in bizarre stunts and fabulous feats.

"I must have been about fourteen or fifteen when I stumbled on *Sideshows by the Seashore*," Rinn recalled. "From that moment on I was hooked. But I never dreamed about trying anything I saw there on my own. In my mind these people had things, or didn't have things that 'normal' people have or don't have, that allow them to perform these odd and unusual acts. Fast forward some twenty or so years, and I see a posting for Sideshow School at Coney Island USA. I had to take the class. I had to know how these feats were done."

An elementary school teacher by day, Rinn found taking on teaching duties along with Vomit enjoyable. "I spend my days dealing with five- to nine-year-olds. Teaching Sideshow School is a huge departure from that. It's a lot of fun. The students at Sideshow School really want to be there, they're not itching to watch *Sponge Bob* and asking to go to the bathroom every five minutes. I've taught people from all walks of life, those that are performers and those that have no intention of ever stepping foot on a stage. Doctors, lawyers, writers, and college students have all gone through the doors of our fine institution.

"It's always great to demonstrate a feat and watch the students' reactions. Usually they have that look that says 'There's no way I'll ever be able to do that.' But guess what, in anywhere from minutes to days they're doing it.

"But the best reactions are the e-mails I get anywhere from a week to a month later. The e-mails thank me for a life-changing experience. Many of my students reflect on the classes as the best time they've had in their lives. And it's not just one or two students who feel this way. Almost every student I've taught has said this."

I suppose that, on some level, it was a life-changing experience I was looking for. And it was a life-changing experience that I got.

CHAPTER TWO

SIDESHOW SCHOOL, DAY ONE: THE HUMAN BLOCKHEAD,

or, How Stupid Do You Think I Am?

Only two things are infinite, the universe and human stupidity, and I'm not sure about the former.

—Albert Einstein

Truth be told, while I attended Sideshow School in April 2007, I first considered attending somewhere around 2003 or possibly 2004. I'd fallen in love with the *Coney Island Circus Sideshow*, had seen the tantalizing Marie Roberts banner on the side of their building that seemed to be screaming SIDESHOW SCHOOL at the top of its lungs to every fiber in my being.

So why the three or four year wait? It had something to do with three little words: Hold Harmless Waiver—and my wife. I was coming from a magic background, which is a world that offers illusion rather than reality, and even if reality was being offered, it was never as it seemed. Rarely was danger a factor.

But Sideshow School was completely different. There is a very real element of danger to nearly every act in the sideshow. You can get hurt. Seriously. All of which gave me pause even before I brought up the subject to my wife as well as the agreement that needed to be signed prior to attending (which states that should you get hurt you will not hold Coney Island USA, your teacher, or any entity involved liable). And after that? Well, that explains the gap of three or four years, doesn't it?

The Hold Harmless Waiver that Coney Island USA requires students to sign brings a definite reality to what you're doing: no more hidden gimmicks, no more sleight of hand. Here was the real deal. Here were skills that if not learned correctly or performed with a modicum of care or caution or both might find you injured.

Part of me was thrilled, not because there was a chance of getting hurt, but because here was an opportunity to learn skills and effects that had nothing to do with deceiving your audience. This seemed like the real deal.

When 2007 rolled around, my family and I had decided to leave New York for Massachusetts. Knowing this, I thought it seemed the right time to strike. So I brought the subject up once again, the rationale being that if I wanted to attend after we moved, I'd end up having to pay for a hotel room to take the course. At least now, while we were still living in New York, I could come home to my own bed every night (the added benefit of having familiar emergency rooms and doctors on hand being left unspoken).

In addition, at first blush these seemed to be a batch of odd and unseemly skills being taught at Sideshow School. Being primarily a children's magician, I'd mentioned what I was doing to a few of the grade school teachers and PTO/PTA parents I'd known from doing school assembly shows in Queens. I was often faced with the same blank, uncertain stare in return, as if they couldn't for the life of them understand why or even how someone would want to do things like this. It was as if someone had punched an unseen cash register button somewhere in their brains and their eyes just came up double "0s." Or the faux smile would appear on their lips, and the disconnected "that's interesting" would be mumbled as they attempted to change the subject. That's when the move to Massachusetts seemed all too right. Once skills such as these are learned, it might be best just to flee the state.

The first day of Sideshow School was cold and miserable. More so being that Coney Island USA is situated only blocks from the boardwalk, with the chill and mist rolling in right off the water. I found a parking space not far from the building. It was late on a Monday morning in April, so the streets were nearly deserted, and Nathan's Hotdogs had only the most rudimentary activity in it thus far. I'd come to know their gastronomic delights and disasters in days to come.

In April of 2007, the building had been promised to Coney Island USA by the city, but Coney Island USA did not yet own it. A major portion of the building was theirs, with the top floor occupied by the Coney Island Museum and the lower floor containing both the sideshow performance space, a tiny cash register, a souvenir shop, and a space they'd deemed "the freak bar." The front corner of the building was still occupied by the government and was used as a U.S. Army Recruiting Station, which seemed both odd and exceedingly bizarre in an almost "this kind of works" sort of way. The square peg didn't fit in the round hole, but given enough military grease and know-how it just might!

On the side of the building is a large orange door through which employees and performers enter in the off-hours. This is no frills. No bell. Just slam your hand against it a few times and hope that someone hears the echo of your request somewhere in the building.

It was cold, and as my fellow classmates gathered that day, we all assumed that the situation probably wouldn't get much better as the week wore on. It being early April, it still felt very much like March, which didn't pose much of a problem until we started learning to breathe fire, but we'll save that for later. Today we're learning the Human Blockhead.

There were plenty of folks in the early part of the twentieth century hammering nails into their noses, but it was Melvin Burkhart who turned the feat into a full-fledged act, adding his own, unique brand of comedy that aided in fleshing out the stunt into something more than a one- or two-minute shocker. Once he honed his routine, it's said that it was Robert Ripley of *Ripley's Believe It or Not* fame who dubbed Melvin the "Human Blockhead." The name stuck not only to Melvin but also to the act itself, wherein a nail is hammered straight into the nose and then removed with little or no harm done to the performer.

Next to Coney Island USA's stage is a tiny dressing room for performers. Another no-frills venue, the room was composed of a small tattered table, dirty mirror, and a trash can. Six of us, which included our instructor, gathered in the small room to learn what it takes to get something up your nose. It turns out, not a lot. But care is needed more than anything.

Care and a little bit of insight and knowledge. I provided the care, since it was my nose, but ultimately the insight and knowledge about where the nail was going was provided by Evan M. Goldman, Ph.D., of Philadelphia University. He led me, step by step, through the channels and ducts that run through our heads and where the nail ultimately goes. Allow me to try to explain.

Most people believe, incorrectly, that when a nail is hammered into the nose, it is actually entering the sinuses. This is both correct and incorrect. The sinuses—or paranasal sinuses—lie above and below the eyes and are usually referred to based on the bones near which they lie.

Let's imagine for a moment that Raquel Welch is in her little ship from *Fantastic Voyage*. Using microtweezers, you carefully place the ship on the tip of a nail and begin hammering said nail into the nose. I know—this is probably the last thing you'd choose to do should you have Raquel Welch at your disposal, but let's run with it nonetheless.

Raquel's in her ship, on the tip of the nail, and she's got a tiny little digital camera clicking away as the nail goes deeper into the nose. The pictures she returns with document the path the nail takes. The first few pictures show the first places the nail passes through, which is a narrow channel known as the nasal cavity. There are two nasal cavities (one leads off from each nostril) that go straight back from the front of the nose to the rear of the head.

The next pictures you find Raquel proudly presenting—as you desperately try to ignore the way her seventies-era jumpsuit clings nicely to her figure—reveal the area where the nasal cavity ends and an area known as the choanae begins. Choanae is plural, and choana would be the singular. At this point, we're still talking about two separate cavities, so there are two choana. However, just a bit farther along the path, as the final pictures show, is the area where the nail's journey ends. Here the two separate channels give way to one larger single space that's referred to as the nasopharynx.

In researching the act, I wanted to know more about where the nail goes and how it's positioned in the head. Maybe an X-ray of my head with the nail inside might be illuminating. I mean, how hard can it really be to get an X-ray of your head on request?

After having done it, all I have to say is, trust me, it might actually have been easier to get Raquel Welch at your disposal than to get an X-ray taken of your head.

Luckily and coincidentally, a friend of mine, Winston Wolf (name changed to protect the innocent), was actually attending school to receive his certification to become an X-ray technician. He suggested that I come down to New York City one weekend and try to get it done on a Sunday afternoon.

Now, my sister, Deb, who at one time was an X-ray technician but was now an ultrasound technician, worked in a hospital herself, but was unable to pull off the miracle of getting me an x-ray of my head. When I found this out, morale hit an all time low. I then asked just about every medical professional I knew, no one could come up with anything. I briefly thought about going to an emergency room with the nail firmly in my nose, claiming ignorance about how it got there and begging for an X-ray. Too many specifics and variables that were out of my control forced me to nix this idea.

So it was that I headed to New York City hoping Winston would be able to deliver. But when Sunday morning gave way to Sunday afternoon and I hadn't heard from him, I began to worry. Finally, late Sunday afternoon, I received a call from Winston. Unfortunately, the site he was familiar with was being manned that day by folks he didn't know. "But," he said, "we might be able to pull it off on Monday if you can stick around." I threw caution to the wind and agreed to stay the extra day.

Hoping to hedge my bets, I decided to attempt one other venue while waiting. While living in New York City my wife and I never had our own doctor (we reeked of stupidity in our youth, but we were rarely sick, what do you want?), so we came to use a little place we'd come to refer to as Doc-in-the-Box, which offered immediate medical care if needed. We'd gone there several times, and they'd even gotten my wife through a bout of pneumonia. They knew us there, and given the fact that they'd been able to diagnose the pneumonia, I knew they had an X-ray machine on the premises since they'd given her a chest X-ray. With time on my hands, I turned to them for the precious image.

It was late Sunday afternoon, and the waiting room was more crowded than I expected it to be. I went to the nurse's station where patients are asked to sign in and explained my situation, telling her that I was working on a book and wanted to get an X-ray of my head as part of the research. Given my track record, I thought it wise to leave out the part regarding the nail until I was actually standing in front of a machine wearing a lead apron. There was no sense in coming off like a complete nut case—at least not right away.

After listening to my plea, the nurse gave me an odd sort of look, then disappeared into one of the offices to discuss my request with one of the doctors. She stood in the doorway of the office. I could see the nurse, but the doctor was still out of sight. Actually I could only hear bits and pieces of the conversation, and one side of it at that. "X-ray...book...research"—shrug and shake of the head—"another Sunday."

The nurse returned to the station and told me the doctor would be out in a moment. I looked around, the eyes of several people, all of them sick or injured, were on me. I felt I'd made a mistake at that point. Even if I received a yes from the doctor, I'd be taking away the staff's time from these people, who were legitimately ill, for my own ridiculous reasons. But that didn't stop me from waiting. What can I say? I wanted that X-ray.

The doctor eventually came out. She was in her late forties and cut to the chase by giving me a *no* right from the start.

"We can't do an X-ray for cases like this. If you ever came down with cancer, we could be held liable."

Liable, a word that would pop up every now and then, nearly haunting me. I nodded and told the doctor I completely understood. Then she made the mistake of asking me what the book was about. I explained it to her, eventually getting to the nail. At first she seemed interested, but as I went on, her face didn't take on the surprised, unsure, or frightened look. Instead, she looked more and more appalled, not so much by the act itself, but, rather, with me as a person. When I finished, she just nodded and turned away with a disgusted "good luck with *that!*" Being a loyal customer anywhere doesn't count for anything these days. And so much for the customer always being right. So, my fate was left in the hands of Winston Wolf.

While working to get his X-ray certification, Winston held down another job. So Monday was spent burning time and trying to figure out what I was going to do if Winston didn't come through. It was late in the day when I went to meet him, and I was pleased to see that he was upbeat about the X-ray happening that day. We went to the site where he'd done some X-ray training.

As we pulled into the parking lot, I noted the sign. It was a women's clinic. Beggars can't be choosers. It was now early evening, and the place was, for the most part, closed. We went downstairs and the two X-ray techs who were wrapping up for the day were more than happy to help, given Winston's ability to grease the social wheels. Liability be damned!

Winston threw a lead apron on me. "Protects the nads," he commented, and positioned me in front of the machine. I jammed the nail home, and somewhere in this book should be a shot of the X-ray that was taken—my proudest moment.

What's shocking is that many people, my sister included, thought the shot was gaffed (rigged). She thought they'd in some way positioned the nail on my cheek. Someone else thought it was Photoshopped. Luckily, two X-rays were taken: one taken in profile and one taken directly head-on. The lateral or profile X-ray shows the path of the nail through the nasal passage, into the choana, and finally into the nasopharynx. The other picture reveals the head of the nail as it goes into the head, making it quite clear that the nail wasn't sitting on my cheek.

Giving it some thought, it probably would've been more difficult to have gaffed and faked the whole thing than to do it for real. Besides, if we'd faked it, I never would've been able to walk away with the thrilling taste of metal in my mouth from the nail. Baskin needs to add a new flavor. They could call it Blockhead. Mint Chocolate Chip with a hint of iron or copper.

After my first day of Sideshow School, I came home to show my wife, to her chagrin, what I'd learned about shoving things in my head, using a Q-tip (not the recommended use for such a product by any physician whatsoever, but I'm sure the same could be said of a nail by a contractor). While she was abhorred by what I'd done, it wasn't long after that she began using something called a Neti Pot to clean out the same areas in her head that I'd been probing. The Neti Pot is a small pot that looks remarkably like a tiny ceramic teapot. You fill it with warm water along with a harmless, salt-based cleansing solution sold with the pot. While leaning over a sink, the water is poured up one nostril and comes pouring out the other. It follows the path we've outlined, going along the nasal cavity and ending up in the nasopharyx. With no place else left to go, it drains out the other nasal cavity, thus the reason why it's good to do something like this over a sink.

Now, of course, anyone who has ever used a Neti Pot or anyone who's ever used any sort of nasal spray or saline solution in the nose knows (see what I did there, witty, no?) there is actually another escape route out of the nasopharyx other than the alternate nasal cavity. Personally, I like to refer to this ancillary route as the Charles Bronson *Great Escape* Route. But before we get to a full explanation of it, allow me to enlighten you with the ways in which sideshow performers have taken Melvin Burkhart's brilliant little routine and expanded on it and expanded on it and expanded on it.

You might be thinking at this point, how much more could possibly be done in an act where a nail is shoved into the head? The truth is, quite a bit. Because once you realize you can get a nail into that space, it soon becomes a sort of strange addiction to find out exactly what else you can get up there.

Sideshow performer extraordinaire Harley Newman (much more on him later) has removed most of the covering from a woman's stiletto heel, leaving the ultrathin, very nasty spike visible. He tips back his head and slides it home. Insert domineering woman joke here.

Two performers I've seen, Donny Vomit of the *Coney Island Circus Sideshow* and Danny Borneo of the *Olde City Sideshow* take a power drill and insert the spinning bit into their heads. Donny particularly milks the effect for every ounce of entertainment value by giving his moustache a stroke and a twist before inserting the drill and then allowing his eyes to go as wide as dinner plates as it vanishes into his head. Next he places the microphone as close to the drill's motor as possible. This enhances the experience for the audience, giving the entire experience a surreal quality, as if you've stepped into some bizarre, real-life showing of the 1979 B horror film *The Driller Killer*. He keeps the bit going deeper and deeper and deeper, and all the while you're fully expecting blood to pour out along the bit's length, running down in swirling rivulets in time with the bit's spinning. But it never does. Each of them drives the bit in and out of his* head with amazing precision. Some would say with more than a few ounces of stupidity as well, but knowing the science behind the act reveals that it's all perfectly safe. Right? Right?

As I've come to learn, the only person who can deem anything safe or not, dangerous or not, or stupid or not is the person holding the drill. When I was first asked to put a nail up my nose, my initial response was, "How stupid do you think I am?" Yet, you overcome that. And the person who picks up that drill might have a fair amount of stupidity in many people's eyes, but you can bet they've more wits about them than you'd expect. You'd have to in order to do the effect safely in the first place.

Gwyd the Unusual of the *Knotty Bits Sideshow* out of Michigan performs another variation of Melvin Burkhart's blockhead routine. Gwyd and his partner, Sylver Fyre, have put together a stunning show, with the perfect balance of humor and edge-of-your-seat excitement. The structure of their show hangs on what seems to be Gwyd enduring and being the sub-

---

* I realize that performers are as likely to be female as male, but in the interest of avoiding awkward constructions such as "he or she," male singular pronouns have been used when applicable.

ject of one excruciating act and seemingly painful act after another as Sylver, her brilliantly striking red hair and figure almost as eye-catching as the act that's being performed, smiles all the while. It seems the type of relationship forged in a BDSM* club, yet the duo have none of the trappings that might be found in an over-the-edge, blood and gore sadomasochistic presentation. In fact, aside from the occasional innuendo, their show is downright family-friendly as well as being exciting.

Gwyd caught my attention at *Sideshow Gathering* (more on this unusual convention much later) when he performed the Blockhead act using the story of King Arthur's Sword in the Stone as the framework. I'm a closet King Arthur-phile, so the presentation immediately caught my attention. But what was truly original and unique is that rather than a common nail, he had a tiny sword forged for just that purpose. Now, you've got to ask yourself, where does one go to get a tiny sword forged to shove up your nose? The answer: The Great Nippullini.

Nippullini, or "Nipps" to his friends, is a retired sideshow performer, but don't let that mislead you. He may be retired, but he's not old enough to sit home and collect Social Security. At just twenty-nine, he works for his family's business, Warrior Body Piercing on South Street in Philadelphia.

While he was doing his act, other sideshow performers may have considered him a one-trick pony in that he really only performed one act and one act only, but he mastered it to the point that it was both cringe worthy and awe inspiring.

What did he do? His name says it all. He lifted and pulled things with the use of his nipples: anvils, bowling balls, and shopping carts with people in them. You name it, Nipps did it, and he holds two world records for it. It all started innocently enough with Nipps watching some videos of pierced weight lifting.

"I've been doing body piercing for fifteen years. I'm a ca-

---

* Bondage and Dominance, and Masochism.

reer piercer. I'm not in it for the scene. If you named famous tattoo artists and piercers, I would have no idea what you're talking about. I don't care about that. If I do a pierce, it's because I'm getting paid for it. So when I heard about pierced weight lifting and saw some video clips of people doing it, I was looking at it and thought, 'You know, something's not right.' Based upon the jewelry size on the performer, the chains they were using—they were obviously plastic—and the weights that they were picking up, the weights this guy was lifting were obviously gaffed. And I thought that's fine and all, but I can do it better."

Being a piercer, Nipps was familiar with not only nipple piercing but also the nipple, what it's composed of, and what it's capable of doing—or what someone would be capable of doing to it.

"Nipple skin is slightly different than all other skin," Nipps said. "It's a sebaceous gland. That's why it's pink. It has extra oil glands in it, and what that does is it helps keep the nipples lubricated. I know that sounds crazy, but that's how God made us. We're made like this, and the main reason why is that geneticists call this the cookie cutter. When we're in the womb, we're all the same. It's like a cookie cutter and primarily we're all female. So because of the fact that in the womb we don't know if we're going to be male or female, you had better come with the stuff that you need to continue existence. So if I was going to be a female, I should have nipples. It turns out that I wasn't, but I still have them. And women's nipples definitely need to be sebaceous glands. They need that to keep them from cracking and chafing so that they don't have problems when it comes to childbirth and feeding. So, yeah, nipples are weird things."

After hanging small items from his nipples in the shop including key clips and metal springs, Nipps finally found something that would bring his feat to another level.

"One of the first things I did, one day when I was working

in the shop down on South Street, I look in the back alley, and there's a shopping cart. So I thought, 'Let's have fun here.' So I get one of the guys that runs the tattoo shop next door. He's a big heavy guy, around 250 or 300 pounds. And I put him in the cart, and I just started pulling him up and down South Street. It was stopping traffic and it was fun, lots of fun. So we're doing this and I look over and there's this art student taking pictures of buildings and stuff, and she said, 'Can I take your picture?' So I said, 'Sure, fine.' So she starts taking pictures of me pulling this fat guy in a shopping cart. Two weeks later I get a package delivered to the shop that says TO THE GUY WHO PULLS THINGS WITH HIS NIPPLES. At that point I didn't have a stage name, and that actually kind of kicked off the name because it had the word 'pull' in it and 'nipples,' and that's really where 'Nippullini' comes from."

Nippullini began his performing career at the *Philadelphia Fringe Festival.* At first he didn't even bother scripting anything, with his only goals being to lift or pull things with his nipples and be funny, both of which he found he was adept at naturally. But after a bit, he decided to script what he was doing. He did so with certain things in mind.

"The script is all based around the props that I'm using. And when I'm selecting a prop that I'm going to lift, it has to fall into three specific categories: The first is that it must be easily recognized by the layperson. They have to be able to look at it and say, 'Oh, I know what that is.' And not only do they know what it is, but they also must be able to say to themselves, 'Man that thing's heavy,' and they *know* it's heavy, for example, a bowling ball. Everyone knows what a balling ball is; they know that's a heavy thing.

"The second thing is it must be heavy. It can't be faked either. It's got to be something you look at and you go, 'There's no way that can't be a heavy item.'

"And the third thing, it has to be something that I incorporate a joke about, for example, my anvils, which is one of my favorites, and it's my trademark, I'm the only person who lifts anvils with nipples. Today. In the 1930s, there was a performer named Rasmus Neilsen who was a blacksmith, and he was a fully tattooed man and he lifted anvils with his nipples. When I found out and I did research about him, I was amazed at that and thought, 'I've got to get me a bunch of anvils.'"

Obviously, unlike hammering a nail into your skull, which, admittedly, can be disconcerting, the act of lifting something with your nipples certainly has a level of pain that some other acts do not have.

"When you're dealing with these kinds of acts, you've got to stop thinking about pain and think more about endurance," Nipps said. "Some of the performers say they get into a Zen state or whatever. I'm not going to fill you with a bunch of bullshit and tell you that I meditate and I do this and I do that. There's a right and wrong way to do everything, and as long as you do it the right way, you'll be alright. The pain, when I'm picking up heavy stuff, the closest that I can equate it to, and that the general public can understand, is if you've ever worked out and done ten or twenty reps of a really heavy weight and all of a sudden you feel this burn. That's lactic acid building up in your muscles, and that burn is the closest thing that I can say, 'That's what it feels like when I pick up something.'"

Now, there are quite a few people out there doing similar acts, some using gaffs or items that aren't really as heavy as they look. But Nipps worked "gaffless," and his act was clearly in the vein of "what you see is what you get." There was no deception or subterfuge, just a guy doing lots of nasty things with his nipples.

In meeting people who performed sideshow acts, one of the questions I usually asked was if they were ever injured while performing. Nipps had the distinction of having one of the more visceral of these tales.

He'd come up with a routine based on Newton's Cradle.

You may not recognize the name, but nearly everyone is familiar with Newton's Cradle. It's the item you usually see in someone's office: four small steel balls hanging by wires. When you lift the ball on the right and let it drop, it hits the next balls, which, in turn, causes the ball all the way to the left to bounce off from the others. That ball comes back down, causing the ball on the right to bounce out, and so on, and so on.

Nipps came up with a version where three sixteen-pound bowling balls were suspended from chains hanging from his nipples. The idea was the two outer balls would be lifted and dropped simultaneously, and when they each simultaneously hit the center ball, the force would cause the two balls to bounce back out continuously, bouncing and clacking against the center ball again and again.

Nipps performed the stunt twice. However, he performed it successfully only once. Every performer, whether it be magicians, sideshow performers, or comedians, is constantly looking for ways in which to include audience members in their act. In this case, Nipps decided to have two members of the audience join him onstage. These two audience members would be the ones to lift the outer balls and drop them simultaneously, thus starting the bouncing motion that was indicative of Newton's Cradle.

The first time he performed the routine it worked beautifully, with both participants dropping the balls at just the right time. The second time he performed it, however, one of the two audience members got the timing wrong and dropped the ball too late, causing the weight of the balls to shift. Gravity came into play, with one ball dropping later than the other. The result was a torn nipple: the trials and tribulations of the sideshow.

But don't be mistaken, that wasn't the reason for his retirement. In fact, his nipples are as strong as ever. When I met him at Warrior Body Piercing, he was more than happy to strap on a fifty-five pound anvil and lift it off the ground. All thanks to those super strong nipples. "I bill myself as the man with the world's strongest nipples," Nipps said. "Currently I'm the only person on this planet that has pulled a car with nipple piercings."

What eventually drove him from the sideshow business was a combination of things.

"I retired for a whole bunch of different reasons. I felt like I wasn't getting what I deserved financially and publicitywise. I was a victim of theft (I put down a little wad of cash backstage and it was gone; then someone took off with one of my stage props), and I even had a show idea stolen from me by, at the time, somebody I thought was a friend here in Philadelphia. I had a great sideshow idea in Philly that never existed, and I had an accident, my nipple tore out and I was out of the scene. Six months later, I'm back in the scene and I find out that the guy I confided to went ahead and ran off with my show idea.

"Another time I got passed over for a gig that I had year after year after year and nobody gave me any explanation. There's a lot of bullshit going on, and I was just like you know what, this is not worth it to me especially when as a performer, on a Saturday, you'd have your big gig, where for me I could do twenty to thirty piercings on a Saturday. That's a big commission day for me. For me to turn that away to go up to New York, spend all this money and do a show, and hardly get anything to come back with, it's not worth it and it's not fun anymore. At one point, it was fun and it still is fun. I definitely do miss the stage. I miss being up there, seducing the audience, having a good time, freaking people out. It's very alluring, but you know, I've got a mortgage, I've got things in my life that are important to me. My job counts."

In addition to piercing bodies and lifting things with his nipples, Nipps is also an extremely talented and gifted blacksmith. One of those rare people with a charm that catches you off guard, he would deny being an artist. But after seeing some of his steel sculptures and what he does with a blow-torch and scrap metal, there is no denying that is just what he is. And it was to Nipps who Gwyd the Unusual went when it came time to find someone to forge him a tiny sword to shove up his nose.

Most sideshow performers use your typical nails found in almost any hardware store. As someone who's shoved a variety of nails into his nose knows (see, I did it again), the hardware store nail is great for a quick fix. But there are problems with them. First, you have to find one long enough. Too short and you may lose the nail in there, and you don't want to do that. The other problem inherent with hardware store nails are burrs, tiny little imperfections in the nail that when the nail is put into your nose it feels more like a hacksaw has been placed in there. And that's where Nipps comes in. Nipps forges nails specifically for the sideshow performer. He doesn't gaff them in any way. These are real nails, but he forges them out of surgical-grade stainless steel, making it the best and safest thing to put in your head. As Gwyd the Unusual remarked, "It's the nicest thing you will ever stick up your nose."

What Nipps did was use the same surgical-grade stainless steel to forge a tiny sword that really is a thing of beauty, with a blade that has a mirror finish, a brass guard, and a handle hand wrapped in stainless steel wire. Again, *that's* the nicest thing you will ever stick up your nose. And while it may be tiny, it rounds out and completes Gwyd's already great King Arthur routine beautifully.

Civilized human beings would say to themselves, "Surely *that's* as far as they can take it. Surely there's nothing more that can be done with and to the little area behind the nose."

Not true. If there's anything I've learned from the sideshow performers I've met, they're only limited by their own imaginations and the wherewithal to push themselves where others fear to tread. I'm sure there are dozens if not hundreds of people out there performing the Human Blockhead routine, each with their own unique spin. But there's one person who's done something just a little bit different with it, and that's Todd Robbins. We'll be learning more about Todd, one of the premiere sideshow performers living today, in a moment. But let's just take a look at what he's done with the Human Blockhead routine.

A friend of Melvin Burkhart prior to his passing, Todd has crafted an exceptionally fine Human Blockhead routine that gives a bit of history to the stunt, pays homage to Melvin, and then takes the whole thing one step further. If you ever have a chance to see him perform it, go out of your way to see it. If you never have the chance to see him perform it, try doing a search for him on YouTube. Maybe, just maybe, the video of him will still be there.

After hammering one of the largest nails I've ever seen into his head, Todd continues his Blockhead routine by turning his attention to a balloon, the kind you'd find clowns making balloon animals out of at a child's birthday party. He partly inflates the balloon and then ties off the end. After generously lubricating the narrow end with a fair amount of saliva, he feeds that end up his nose—which brings us conveniently back to the Charles Bronson *Great Escape* Route. Just to recap, if you insert something laterally into the nose, it'll go through the nasal cavity, through the choana, and end up in the nasopharynx. And if you're like my wife and use a Neti Pot, the liquid poured into one nasal passage will make its way down to the nasopharynx and then find its way out via the other nasal passage. However, there is another way out, and that's what I've come to call the Charles Bronson *Great Escape* Route.

Let's go back to a boring old nail for a moment. When you insert a nail into your nose, in addition to the very bizarre experience of having something like that in your head where you normally don't have anything, there's also something else: something extra, something quite strange.

You see, when you shove a nail into your nose, you can *taste* it. You can taste the nail just as if you stuck it in your mouth and sucked on it. It all has to do with the way in which the nose and the mouth are positioned, one literally on top of the other, and the fact that the two senses are so closely interrelated. Ever have a cold so bad you lose all sense of not just smell but taste as well? That's because they're connected, both figuratively and literally.

So when my wife uses the Neti Pot, most of the liquid ends up pouring out of the other nasal passage, but some of the liquid actually can leak down and find its way into her mouth (postnasal drip, anyone?) using the Charles Bronson *Great Escape* Route.

It's also what happens when Todd feeds the end of a balloon up his nose. The balloon travels along the nasal cavity, eventually ending up in the nasopharynx. It's there that rather than bending and going into the other nasal cavity (which for a liquid is easy, but for a solid, not so much so), if it's properly lubricated, it will pass into the oropharynx, cross the fauces, which is the opening at the back of the mouth, and drop down into the mouth.

Check out Todd's performance. He feeds the narrow end of the balloon up his nose, then reaches into his mouth to retrieve it. I'll spare you the detail of him forcing the air from one end of the balloon to the other through his head. It's too much a thing of beauty. It almost brings tears to your eyes.

At first, when you hear that you'll be shoving things into your nose like nails, screwdrivers, and ice picks, you really want to ask the person suggesting it, "How stupid do you think I am?" And oftentimes when I've played with the stunt, licking a nail and sliding it into my head, I often imagine hearing the *Three Stooges* theme in the background. But, ultimately, what I'm doing, being the blockhead that I am, is really not so much exploiting my own stupidity as much as the stupidity and ignorance of others. It looks like a stupid stunt when, in fact, what you're doing is exploiting the lack of knowledge on the audience's part. Few people realize that this can be done, and done safely, by most anyone.

The question is, would most people want to do it? I thought yes. I thought wrong.

I was invited to a party aptly dubbed RobCon. Held once a year, my friend Tom was invited, and in turn asked the host, Rob Trimarco (the Rob of RobCon), if I might tag along.

What more can you say about RobCon other than it's a geek's paradise. Held in early September while the weather was still warm, Rob's backyard was filled with tables at which twenty-sided dice were being rolled and ninth-level Wizards ruled the world. In addition to the token Dungeons & Dragons table, there were other tabletop games being played as well, including Arkham Asylum and a mini combat game called Monster-pocaclypse.

Inside, more geek fun was being had as a widescreen television was used for Guitar Hero. Here the complete band was set up, with one player at guitar, one at bass, another on drums, and a singer holding the microphone rounding out the faux band as they cranked their way through song after song, attempting to gain the admiration of a virtual crowd that cheered them on.

Since Rob had been kind enough to invite me, I returned in kind by bringing along some bottles of Coney Island Ale as well as offering to perform something. Now, as I've been told, Tom mentioned that I was a magician, which might well explain some of the reactions to what I did. If you expect a card trick and get something that's decidedly *not* a card trick, well, that can throw you for a loop.

What I decided to perform was the Human Blockhead. I'd put together a brief presentation using a Philips head screwdriver and a nail. A small group of people gathered in the yard, and as I performed it, I took in each stunned face. Most were aghast, and I think others were still convinced what they were seeing was, in fact, some sort of trick or deception.

In the end I offered to teach anyone who wanted to learn it, how to do it—safely. I had not a single taker, so my friend Tom volunteered, but got no further than getting the item offered a few millimeters into his nose before being hit by a tremendous sneezing fit, a common reaction to expect for first-time blockheads.

But that evening certainly answered my question. Yes, anyone *can* do it. Would anyone want to? Apparently not, which struck me as an oddity. I'd fully expected most people to want to try something like this. I expected people to be willing to take the leap and try something new, something that few people knew was possible, but, in reality, is within the grasp of most everyone. But this wasn't the case.

Disappointment raced through me that evening, not only partly in myself for possibly not having presented the effect properly, but also mainly in the people I presented it to. Were people less daring than I thought? Had I presented a fool's errand and, thus, made their decision for them, nullifying any desire they might have had to try something unique and different? From where did the error stem? I knew that, for various reasons, I'd wanted to learn these skills, and part of that reason was to sort of throw caution to the wind. Maybe, for some, caution to the wind was too much.

〜〜

CHAPTER THREE

THE FREAKOPHILES PRESENT TODD ROBBINS:

Charlatan, Con Man and Freak— Alive on the Inside!

I wanted to see real magic. I didn't want to see tricks, I wanted to see real magic...and the guy swallowing swords, the guy eating fire, the guy hammering a nail into his nose; it hit me that these were not tricks, and it not only amazed me but filled me with a desire to learn how to do this.
—Todd Robbins, sideshow performer

If he so desires, Todd Robbins can be both imposing and intimidating. His height allows him to dwarf others easily, yet his charm, his likeability, and the manner in which he makes anyone feel immediately at ease is disarming.

Yet through the charm and friendly exterior, there is one thing that surfaces more than anything, the one thing that seems to exude from Todd's every pore: his sheer and unadulterated love of the sideshow. In addition to being an exemplary performer, he also retains an almost encyclopedic knowledge of not only the skills and stunts found in the sideshow but also the rich and abundant history behind it. That's not to say his own history is less than rich and abundant.

"The story is, I grew up in Southern California," Todd began. "And that, for many people who know Southern California, is reason enough why I would want to hammer a nail into my nose. But it's a little bit different. It's an old story of the darkness of suburbia, and that's why there's rampant drug use and why in these lovely upscale communities there are kids putting together a punk rock band or a grunge band in their garage, because it's a little bit of rebellion. And for me it wasn't really rebellion as it was that I just love character, I love things that stimulate and challenge a little bit.

"And everything was manufactured in suburbia. It was tract homes and everything looked planned, and the lawns and the landscape and everything, and it was a place that sort of persistently insisted that this was not a way of life, but *the* way of life. This was the American dream."

Todd grew up in this faux Stepford environment with not so much a need to rebel as to fill what seemed to be a hole in his life. He was unsure of what would fill that hole, but the answer soon came in the discovery that a magic shop had opened in town. And with that, Todd's world changed.

"A magic shop opened in our neighborhood. Outside of the neighborhood, in the kind of run-down part that had yet to be torn down and gentrified, there was an old little seedy strip mall that a magic shop opened in, and I thought this was the greatest news ever, the idea of a magic shop. So I finally convinced my mom to take me to it, and I was about ten years old. And we went in there. And she was a little bit horrified by the place, and I just thought it was the greatest thing. Even though it wasn't that old, it seemed dusty; it seemed like it had been there for thirty years, and it was seedy, no two ways about it. And there was this older German man that looked like Bela Lugosi's brother behind the counter doing magic tricks. It was just great, and I bought a Svengali deck."

The shop, it turned out, offered magic lessons, but before allowing their son to attend, Todd's parents looked into the owner and found out he was an active and respected member of the community.

"His name was Herb Fiedler, and Herb had lived in Germany and worked for the underground and got caught and was put into a concentration camp for a number of years during the war. And he had escaped to Belgium where he didn't speak the language. There were ten of them that escaped and only two survived, and he had a bullet wound in his shoulder. In the town they escaped to, the people wanted nothing to do with them. They wouldn't help them at all because they knew the Nazis would roll in and burn the town down and kill everyone if they found that they were sympathizers.

"So they hid underneath a bridge, and were trying to figure out what to do, and he would go in the town and go through the trash to try to find some food, and he met some of the children and did some sleight of hand for them. And the kids warmed to him, and the adults then saw that he was a good man and they took them in, nursed the two of them back to health, and got them to the underground and got them to the United States." At which point Fiedler returned to Europe to continue his work with the underground. Eventually he made his way back to the United States, and it was in his shop on Saturdays that the magic classes took place.

"He was a great man, and quite an inspiration, and on Saturday afternoons, magicians would hang out in the front room, and they'd sit there and do card tricks for each other and smoke unfiltered Camel cigarettes and swap lies. And I used to go in there and hang around for hours after the magic lessons, and just soak up the stories."

He was twelve or thirteen when a carnival came to his town, and, along with it, a sideshow.

"A carnival came to our neighborhood, it was part of a charity event, and they had a sideshow. It was put together by Jack Waller, and I didn't know who he was. I just went in because the outside talker was talking about the master of magic you're going to see on the inside. And the magic act was so bad I almost left. And it was only years later that I discovered that that's the beginning of the turn, that you have the magic act, so as the crowd's coming in, the guy's doing trick after trick, and he gets the "office" from the ticket taker saying they're all in, then he does the last trick, then he turns it over to the rest of the show. So fortunately I stayed and the rest of the show was exactly what I was looking for, because I wanted to see real magic. I didn't want to see tricks; I wanted to see real magic. That's why I watched so much magic, because I wanted something that wasn't fake. I wanted something real, extraordinary, and with character, like the guy swallowing swords, the guy eating fire, the guy hammering a nail into his nose. It hit me that these were not tricks, and it not only amazed me but filled me with a desire to learn how to do this."

Todd went to the magic shop that afternoon and told the others there where he'd been and that he'd love to find someone to teach him such skills. It turned out that quite a few of the men had done time as carnies or as sideshow workers, and one of them had even worked for the *Pete Cortez Sideshow* for a time and knew how to eat fire and hammer a nail into his nose. Todd was hooked.

But there was a tradition in the sideshow, Todd was told, where you don't just walk in and learn it all, you had to prove yourself first by spending a season taking tickets, sweeping up, and doing the grunt work around the show. Only when you prove you're "with it" may you start to learn such skills.

Being twelve or thirteen at the time, the young Todd wasn't sure how he'd make that happen. Then the man suggested Todd help him out. A magician by trade, it was getting into the holiday season, and he suggested Todd help him with his holiday shows. Todd agreed and from Thanksgiving to New Year's he worked at places like the Elk's Club, the Rotary, and the local hospital. While the magic show was going on, Todd, clad in a clown costume, would make balloon animals for the children at the back of the room. During this period the number of shows climbed to five or six a week, but to the man's surprise, Todd stuck with it. And true to his word, he sat down with him and taught him the first sideshow skills he'd learn, telling him to bring some Q-tips to help him open up his nose and some rags and hangers to make crude beginner torches.

Todd began to pick up skills from various performers. One, Red Garland, performed a human ostrich routine in which he'd swallow items and regurgitate them. He'd swallow cigarettes, pieces of tin cans, and other items. The man even chewed up and swallowed a lightbulb, a skill that immediately caught Todd's attention.

"Red Garland did a human ostrich act in which he ate things. He'd come out smoking a cigarette, and he'd tongue it, bring it up, and do all these things, then he'd swallow it. He'd chew it up and swallow it, then drink water. And he would also bite into a tin can, and he'd eat a lightbulb. He had one big joke in his act where he said, 'I brought a young lady to see me perform one time and I was trying to impress her, so I was doing all that I do. I was eating the cigarettes, and I was chewing on a tin can, and I was eating glass, and afterwards I said, 'What do you think?' And she said 'That's nothing. A goat can do all that and give milk too.' And that was the one joke he had in his act.

"But he showed me how to eat glass. He broke a lightbulb and made me do all the preparation for it, and then said to take this little piece and eat it. He showed me how to chew it, and asked if I was bleeding, and I said, 'No, no, no.' He said,

'Okay, come back next week, and if you're still alive, we'll go further.'"

Todd began to accrue a number of sideshow skills but never actually performed them. He was still young and at the time had aspirations of being a magician or an actor. He eventually got a degree in theater and made his way to the American Conservatory Theater in San Francisco. Here he received some much-needed real-life education from actors who were doing just that, acting. Doing much of the training at the American Conservatory Theater (ACT) were actors who were part of a local theater company. It was a resident company that meant they'd do seven or ten plays and hire the actors for the whole season. They'd often perform in rep, which, in many ways, is as close to a 10-in-1 sideshow as you can get.

"A performer might be playing Scrooge in *A Christmas Carol* at the matinee, then in the evening might have a smaller role in a Shakespeare play," Todd recalled. "Then that same person might be doing a Neil Simon comedy the following week all while rehearsing a David Mamet play" that's on the horizon. In many ways, this was the same grind that Todd had seen at the sideshow, one show following the other following the other.

From these actors, Todd received his training, but the Reagan era had begun and funding for the arts and certainly for local theater troupes was beginning to dry up. To make ends meet, Todd began working comedy clubs with some comedy magic routines, but he came to realize that he needed to make a choice between Los Angeles and New York.

"It seemed," Todd said, "that any longevity in Los Angeles required a theater background, and since New York was the theater capital, then New York it was."

During the 1980s, he worked many comedy clubs in New York and ended up getting a position as an emcee at a club in Greenwich Village called Mostly Magic. Along with a prix fixe meal, the emcee served up a variety act and a headline almost every night. As emcee, Todd would perform a few of the comedy magic routines he'd honed in other clubs.

Then Todd heard about an MTV show looking for something unusual. He'd worked out a routine where he stuck his hand in an animal trap and got to perform the bit. He enjoyed doing it and thought he might use it at Mostly Magic.

"After doing a few other routines, I told the audience that what I'd just done was a trick, but what I was about to do was not."

He then performed the animal trap routine. Along with the performance came a revelation that was instilled in him when he was younger yet came back to him: there was no deception, but the stunt was no less amazing than the magic he'd been performing. He'd stunned the audience, and at that, he slowly began to take the magic out of his routines and add in more sideshow stunts. He presented it out of the context of the sideshow, wearing a suit and framing the stunts as simply strange skills or effects. "I certainly would mention the stunt's sideshow origins, but didn't frame it as such, not coming out in a straw hat or a vest."

In addition, as the magic went out of his act and the sideshow skills went in, Todd came to realize that such feats came with a very strong gross-out factor. These were things that made people squeamish, with some things almost forcing them to cover their eyes and peek through their fingers to watch as if they were at a horror movie. Acknowledging this fact, Todd worked on his routines to play against that, attempting to make the effects as accessible as possible. You do, after all, want your audience to see what you're doing.

Picking up shows at comedy clubs as well as at various colleges, Todd eventually found his way to Coney Island with a friend from ACT who was doing a project on popular entertainment and decided to focus on the famed entertainment hub. It was winter and at the time Coney Island USA was located on the boardwalk. Since it was out of season, the sideshow wasn't in operation, but the Coney Island Museum was open. It was then that he first met Dick Zigun. They had a brief conversation, but it wasn't until a year later that Todd made his way back to see the show.

"When I went, I saw a guy hammering a nail into his nose. And not just a nail, but the biggest assed nail I'd ever seen." And at the same time he was doing this, the man was able to make the audience laugh. The man was Melvin Burkhart. Todd immediately started a friendship with the man and discovered that while Melvin didn't invent the stunt, he was the one who made it into an act.

"This wasn't just a guy, but *the* guy when it came to hammering a nail into the nose." When he came to this realization, Todd mentioned to Melvin that he also did the Blockhead.

"Do you do my routine?" Melvin asked.

"No," Todd responded.

"If you want to you can," was Melvin's response.

But Todd felt he'd stolen something from the man and offered to stop doing the routine if Melvin wanted. But Melvin encouraged him to continue and told him that if there was anything in his routine he wanted to use he was welcome to it. He only requested that he do it well.

It was while performing at colleges that he felt like he should work for a real sideshow if, for nothing else, the experience. He considered Ward Hall's World of Wonders, which was and is still in operation, but touring would be difficult and he enjoyed living in New York. So he approached Dick Zigun and began working the sideshow in Coney Island. He spent many years with them and worked on getting them the building.

It was during Todd's time at Coney Island that Melvin passed away. They'd become fast friends and Melvin's final performance was at Todd's wedding. It was at that point that Todd came to the realization that an entire generation of sideshow performers were being lost, and we were on the verge of losing the next one as well. He spoke to Dick Zigun and suggested the need to start a sideshow school, something where the torch—both literally and figuratively—could be passed and the tradition could be kept alive. And that's what they did, creating a place where not only the skills were taught but also a bit of the history and tradition that went along with them.

Occupying himself with a variety of projects, from Off-Off-Broadway shows to Coney Island to emceeing gigs, Todd found himself at a sort of crossroads in his life.

"My wife had become pregnant. I began to reevaluate things and realized that so much of what I loved about Coney Island just doesn't exist anymore. Much of it seemed like a slum and was overly depressing."

True, there were efforts to improve it, and what it will ultimately become may be truly exciting, but it will never be what it was, and any future it had was out of Todd's hands and out of his control. Having departed from Coney Island, Todd has more irons in the fire than a blacksmith in the Old West. He can often be found emceeing Monday Night Magic in Manhattan. Todd is also working on a show titled *Hoodwinked*, an examination of cons, scams, and swindles, which has seen a handful of performances on the East Coast and seems to be headed for a bright future.

Most recently, Todd began emceeing duties at Magical Nights at Feinstein's at Lowe's Regency. Billed as "exclusive evenings of unforgettable wonder," the five-star elite club offers, in addition to the emcee's ten-minute sets, a close-up magician and a headliner. Todd had brought out a few other routines for this, a different sort of crowd than you'd find in Greenwich Village, but one evening a colleague suggested he try sword-swallowing. He didn't consider it the best room or audience for such a feat, but Todd did a ten-minute set one evening incorporating the stunt and found that not only did it play but it killed (no pun intended)—Which just goes to show that overall, people aren't that different.

So now Robbins is the Park Avenue Sword-Swallower. And the world of the sideshow is a little bit brighter for his existence.

CHAPTER FOUR

~ᗡ

SIDESHOW SCHOOL, DAY TWO: LYING ON A BED OF NAILS,

or, Really, What's the Point?

In physics, you don't have to go around making trouble for yourself—nature does it for you.
— Frank Wilczek

The second floor of *Coney Island USA* houses the Coney Island Museum, a unique collection of memorabilia immortalizing Coney Island's heyday of the early part of the twentieth century when places like Luna Park and Dreamland were living and breathing entities and drew crowds from Manhattan and Long Island with their vast array of entertainment. Thanks to the brilliance of Thomas Edison, Coney Island at the time was electrified, and at night it could be seen for miles away, its lights cutting through the darkness, earning it the name City of Fire.

At the entrance to the museum sits a Kinetoscope, a nostalgic piece of machinery that looks as if its been belched up directly from the 1939 World's Fair in Queens, New York, although the thick layers of paint on it do it no justice.

But it does still accept coins. Drop one in, position your

eyes over the viewer, turn the crank, and watch as the Kineto-scope presents you with a short film. Like much of *Coney Island USA*, the film is a bizarre one, strange beyond belief but just as much a part of history as everything else in the museum.

The film depicts the last moments of an elephant known as Topsy. The year was 1903, and Topsy was a domesticated elephant with the Forepaugh Circus, which had an affiliation at the time with Coney Island's Luna Park. Now it should be noted at the outset that when dealing with an animal the size of an elephant, domestication really is no guarantee for anything. Abuse doesn't help the situation any either.

After being fed a lit cigarette, Topsy killed a man, and it was quickly decided that she be put down. The duties fell to Thomas Edison. If you're ever unsure of what the great men of history did with their leisure time, then it might be suggested that you take a close look at Edison. In his quest to prove that DC current electricity was more stable, viable, and less dangerous than AC current, Edison made use of AC current to electrocute everything from dogs and cats to horses. Children in his neighborhood must have watched him warily while clutching their family pets.

It was Edison's idea that Topsy be electrocuted, and after feeding the elephant carrots laced with cyanide—just to ensure things went smoothly—that's just what happened. Various cables were connected to Topsy's massive feet. They snaked across the ground around her, running through chains and shackles, giving the entire affair the appearance of some strange, medieval torture device.

The quarter dropped into the Kinetoscope will earn you approximately a forty-five-second viewing of Topsy's death as documented by Edison. One moment the pathetic beast is standing upright, the next she is falling to the ground, with billowing tendrils of smoke pouring forth from her feet. It's a sad thing to see, truly, and one of the more bizarre finds among the *Coney Island USA* collection. But after spending a week there, the word "bizarre" really becomes relative.

The Kinetoscope sits at the rear of the room, and we're led to the front where a board is dropped to the floor, its weight obvious from the near deafening crash that resounds around us. The board is approximately fifty-six inches in length, and some twenty-six inches in width. It's depth is no more than a couple of inches, and from it protrudes some one thousand nails, each spaced proportionately so as to provide a modicum of comfort. Though much like the word "bizarre," at *Coney Island USA* the word "comfort" is also relative.

Not surprisingly, the overall look of the bed of nails is much like a medieval torture device in its own right. This one obviously has a bit of age on it. Some of the nails are rusty, some twisted or bent, and others have what seem to be the rotting remnants of food cluttered at the base. Chunks of an apple here or a melon there remain, items used to prove the sharpness of the nails during a performance. Cleaning out this debris would be a fruitless (no pun intended) effort since it resides at the very bottom where the nails protrude from the board, an area that's nearly impossible to reach because of the lack of space between each sharply pointed nail. Three words: cuts, blood, tetanus. Does one *really* need a clean bed of nails? The bits of apples and melons are welcome to stay.

The bed of nails is *not* a one-note act. Like any good sideshow act, it requires a proper presentation, something more than, say, "Here's a bed of nails, watch me lay on it, wasn't that amazing." To flesh out the presentation, a few twists can be added, twists that further exploit the principle behind the bed of nails. One is the introduction of a concrete block and a sledgehammer, similar to the act I'd briefly witnessed as a boy. The usual way this is achieved is the person lying on the nail bed holds a concrete block on his chest while an assistant uses the sledgehammer to break the block. The block shatters, and the person lying on the bed of nails rises unharmed.

Another version introduces spectators or a beautiful assistant into the mix, where one or more people stand on either the chest or other body parts of the person lying down. The result is the same each time. The person rises, his flesh pockmarked from the nails, but not pierced. He is unharmed.

When it comes to be my time to lie on the bed of nails, I slough off my jacket, lower myself to the floor, and bring my back down slowly to meet the tips of the nails. It's a strange sensation at first, because, to be honest, you fully expect there to be some form of pain in what you're doing. This can be true of most acts and skills learned in Sideshow School, but when you're lowering your body onto some one thousand nails, you wouldn't expect anything less, but that's not what you get. Comfort may be relative, but surprisingly I find the bed of nails provides just that. Next to my body, with my fingers, I can feel the nails there; some are like corkscrews, others are bent, and still others so rusted that you can actually feel the corrosion on the length of the nail. And I wonder if the bed of nails I'm lying on is actually as old as the feat itself.

Sideshow performer extraordinaire and someone who does some stunning bed of nails presentations, Harley Newman, briefly outlined the history of the stunt for me. "In the Middle East, thorns were a performance convention for street preachers," Newman said. "People saw some guy lying on thorns in the middle of their village and knew a show was about to happen." Once the crowd had gathered, they'd perform a little sleight of hand, making items appear and disappear, with the gods taking most of the credit. The performer would then do some preaching and even commune with the spirits in ways that we'd associate today more with the work of Jay Johnson, Jeff Dunham, or Terry Fator than John Edward (though the latter might have more in common with the former three than we think, who knows). "It'd end," Newman notes, "with a pitch for amulets, rings, beads, good-luck objects, and fertility symbols."

Newman also makes reference to the Maya culture's Bible, the *Popul Vuh*, which references one of their cultural heroes who happens to be a baby. "As a baby he was unable to sleep unless he was lying on thorns. He also walked on stilts and swallowed 'swords.'" Dakota Fanning eat your heart out! You don't have that much talent in your pinkie toe.

It doesn't take much of a leap to go from beds of thorns to beds of nails, but the point here (pun completely intended) is how old the stunt is, how it's grown and evolved over the years, and how it's been used for more than entertaining sideshow audiences.

India was under British rule for nearly two hundred years. During that time of occupation British soldiers were a constant presence, keeping a grip on the country for the United Kingdom. From these soldiers came a myriad of amazing tales and stories, many of which had their basis in fact. British soldiers witnessed spectacular feats of illusion and magic from the fakirs in India, relaying what they'd seen to others via word of mouth and correspondence. As what they'd witnessed went from one person to the next, exaggeration helped embellish the fact, and the spectacular soon became miraculous.

Indian fakirs presented many a gruesome and sometimes bloody effect. Oftentimes these were performed as proof that their minds had attained power over their bodies. And while some of these effects did, in fact, have their basis in illusion, others—often the more horrifying ones—were, in fact, skills that these street performers had developed, such as fire-eating or sitting and lying on a bed of nails.

Photographer Alfie Goodrich provided me with a stunning photograph of an Indian fakir sitting on a bed of nails taken circa 1915. "It was taken by my paternal grandfather, Cyril Goodrich. He was twenty-one at the time the photo was taken, in 1915, whilst serving with the British Army's 'Machine Gun Corps.' I don't know where it was taken, but grandfather was based in the general vicinity of Jubblepore. Knowing the Army (I once served as well), he probably would not have been allowed to stray too far from base. So I think it is safe to assume that Jubblepore is the general area in which the pic was shot."

Strangely enough, the bed of nails on which the fakir is sitting looks remarkably like the one I had lain on on Coney Island. I can only imagine what it took to create such a prop in 1915. I suppose, if you're a fakir or someone claiming you're able to accomplish amazing feats because of the blessings of god, that might be incentive enough.

Now if anyone tries to sell you on the fact that either sitting on or lying on a bed of nails is in any way, shape, or form proof that he's attained some form of higher consciousness, giving his mind power over the pain and injury inflicted on his body, you should feel free to find a hammer and go to work on his skull. His higher consciousness might suddenly have gone out for a break and is unable to prove itself against the iron weight of a hammer. Okay, don't go after him with a hammer, but feel free to slap him upside his head at least.

In any case, whether the performers in India were aware of it or not, they were utilizing basic principles of physics to achieve what their spectators at the time believed was a mastery of the mind over the body. But it's all physics, as my burger-loving fat ass and I found out. My mind had nothing to do with it.

As I've come to discover thanks to a brilliant physics professor by the name of Daryl Taylor (who is really skilled enough to teach Neanderthals such as myself about concepts that might otherwise never penetrate the cranium and actually makes use of a bed of nails in his AP Physics classes), it takes between four and five pounds of pressure to break the skin. Luckily, this wasn't something I found out the hard way.

In physics there's a little equation that goes something like this: $P = F/A$. That meant about as much to me as $E = Mc^2$. And not that I'm in any way insulting the intelligence of

Indian fakirs, but it'd probably mean even less to them, especially if we were referring to fakirs in the early part of the twentieth century. But the secret to lying on a bed of nails is right there in that equation: P = F/A (pressure = force divided by the area).

Still means a hill of beans, doesn't it? Let me help. Let's start with force. Force is our weight. And there ain't nothing we can do about our weight. Unless you have a militant Susan Powter (wherever you are) cracking a whip and driving you for a month toward the goal of a slender, slim, rocking bod, there's nothing you're going to be able to do to change your weight. So the force is a constant and unchanging.

Let's say, just hypothetically, that you weigh 200 pounds. That's the force. We'll now retire to the kitchen, since it's the scene of the crime and the place where most of this "force" has come from. If you weigh 200 pounds, then when you're standing up in your kitchen, your feet are putting 200 pounds of force on your linoleum floor. That 1 square foot of space that your feet take up on the floor is receiving 200 pounds of force.

Now let's change things up a bit. If you lie down on your kitchen floor, then you're still putting 200 pounds of force on the floor, but the *area* has increased. You've spread out that 200 pounds. Rather than placing the force of 200 pounds onto 1 square foot of the floor when you're standing on it, you've now spread your weight out over a larger area of the floor.

Okay, hypothetical kitchen time is over. Grab the box of donuts that you've been keeping in your fridge for a snack, and let's move on over to our hypothetical sideshow stage where our bed of nails is waiting for us. Polish off the box. We'll pretend that even after that snack your weight remains at 200 pounds.

Let's assume, for a moment, that we're masochists, and we've made a bed of nails out of 10 nails. If we were to lie down on that bed of nails, then our 200 pounds would be spread out over those 10 nails, putting 20 pounds of pressure on each nail.

Remember what I said earlier? It takes between four and five pounds of pressure to break skin. So guess what, that 10-nail bed of nails you've made is sure to turn you into a human shish kabob just in time for your next barbecue. Combine this tragic mistake with a few of the mistakes you could make while eating fire and your barbecue could potentially be featuring shish kabob and fondue all made out of you! Your friends and family will love it. Fun for all!

And if you still don't get the message, let me put it out there loud and clear: sideshow skills are dangerous. Let me repeat that, sideshow skills are dangerous! We're dealing with science here, and if the science isn't right, then something bad will happen. What happens when NASA doesn't get their science right? The shuttle explodes. What happens if you don't get your science right? You could get seriously hurt. So get your science right.

You want to make sure that your hypothetical 201 pounds (okay, I'm penalizing you for the donuts) is spread out over a large area. Once you increase the area, then the pressure goes down. Let's try another scenario. Let's assume, once again, that you weigh 201 lbs. because, remember, that's a constant, and you can't change it. Now, let's assume that you've made your bed of nails out of 200 nails. What's the force or weight being put on each nail? One pound?

You've increased the area on which your weight lies; therefore, the pressure reduces to one pound of force per nail. Not enough to break skin, but enough to give you a nice pock-marked look, like you've just gone a round or two with Pinhead from Clive Barker's *Hellraiser*.

So remember, less nails means that the pressure will increase because the area has decreased. This is bad. More nails means that the pressure will decrease because the area has increased. This is good. The force remains the same because you can't change your weight. Therefore, in order to change the pressure, you have to change the area. The area, which is the nails, is what you're controlling. So take control of it.

Now, the preceding explanation is completely hypothetical. I would not, under any circumstances, suggest you build a bed of nails using two hundred nails. You want to hedge your bets and make sure that the bed of nails you build will be not only good for you but perfect for you or anyone else who might happen along and want to catch a few z's on it. How do you hedge those bets? Increase the nails, increase the nails, increase the nails. Increase the area by insane numbers, and you'll be safer than a blind man wandering aimlessly in a Sleepy's store.

After Sideshow School, I built my own bed of nails. I started with two pieces of plywood. Both had the same dimensions: approximately 48″ x 28″. This gave me a significantly large enough bed to lie down on. The first piece of plywood was 1/2″ thick. The second piece of plywood was 1/4″ thick.

On the first piece of plywood I drew a grid. First, I made marks down the length of the board every 3/4″. Then I went across the width of the board making marks every 3/4″. Finally, using a yardstick as a guide, I connected all those markings with lines, creating my nail grid. The result was a grid where each line was exactly 3/4″ apart—no more than that. Less is better, so if you can do less, do it. Make yourself a grid that's made up of lines 1/2″ apart if you want. That's safer because you're increasing the area since you'll be using more nails. But a comfortable bed should have a 3/4″ grid on it.

Now the hard part: where each line intersected, I hammered a nail. Since I was anal about my grid, each nail ended up being no farther than 3/4″ apart from one another.

Remember, we're dealing with science here. If you're off, then you very well might injure yourself. I made sure that those nails were kept close together and were not hammered into the board in any haphazard way. They followed the grid I'd marked out earlier.

One thing I did was leave a 1″ border all the way around the board, so there were no nails there. You want to be able to pick the bed of nails up eventually, and you certainly can't do that if every portion of the board is covered in nails.

Once I successfully covered the entire board with nails, I took my second piece of plywood and put it up against the side where the nail heads were exposed. Basically, I sandwiched the heads of the nails between two boards. I took some screws, twelve of them, and screwed the two boards together along the 1″ border I left behind. Ultimately, what this sandwiching did was prevent the nails from becoming loose or falling out. Since the heads of the nails were now up against another board, they had nowhere to go. Finally, at one end of the board I affixed a block of wood that ran the width of the board. I then found a handle and screwed it directly into the wood, which made the bed of nails much easier to transport.

Remember, science doesn't lie. It doesn't. It just doesn't. There's no getting around it or the math. If the math tells you that 10 nails will exert 10 pounds of pressure on a 200-pound human being, or even a 201-pound human being, then the math also tells us that those 10 nails are going to be breaking skin and may even end up causing severe injury.

One performer apparently wanted to make his bed of nails more perilous than others, and spaced the nails on the bed 3″ apart. The goal here was to make the stunt look much harder and more difficult than it was. While it's true that the bed of nails, if properly built, isn't that difficult to perform, trying to make it seem harder by way of forcing the hand of science is a futile effort at best. The performer did walk away from his nail bed, but ultimately was more the worse for wear as each pockmark in his back became a bloody puncture wound.

While science doesn't lie, you need to expand your thinking and extrapolate the findings into some commonsense conclusions. Yes, you can't change science, and lying on a bed of nails isn't that difficult. Does that mean, then, that you can jump up and down on it, throw yourself on it, or perform some other insane feat? Probably not.

But if there's any doubt that something new and different can be brought to such an old stunt, think again. After attending *Sideshow Gathering* and watching performer after performer put their own spin on the bed of nails, you get a sense that almost anything can be done if you have a powerful enough imagination.

The most memorable bed of nails performance I witnessed was by Tyler Fyre and Thrill Kill Jill of the *Lucky Daredevil Thrill Show*. Billing the routine as *The Chainsaw Picnic*, Jill lies down on the bed of nails and holds a pumpkin on her stomach. As she lies there, Tyler uses a chainsaw to cut the pumpkin in half. The stage is showered in bits of pumpkin as the sound of the chainsaw fills the room. It's a slow process cutting a pumpkin with a chainsaw while taking care not to cut the person on which it is lying, but slow is good. If the routine is quick, then the anticipation and suspense would evaporate, leaving it much less satisfying. As it is, the slow cutting of the pumpkin leaves the audience on the edge of its seat, wondering if Tyler might go just a bit too far this time and cut into Jill's abdomen. No one would actually say that, but with many sideshow routines, that's surely the unspoken thoughts of many audience members. There's real danger here. The potential for harm is only moments and the slip of the wrist away. The danger being the potential for harm is one of the reasons why we watch.

Ultimately, dealing with a bed of nails is a lot like playing football with a porcupine as the ball. It can be done, but it takes an incredible amount of respect and finesse to refine your handling in the ultimate goal of not getting yourself hurt.

No matter how simple the feat, there's always the chance that you could get hurt. So set aside your ego, keep your wits about you, make sure your science is correct, and lie down with respect.

If you respect the bed of nails when lying down, then chances are that in the morning the bed of nails will respect you.

◁~◁~◁

CHAPTER FIVE

THE FREAKOPHILES PRESENT HARLEY NEWMAN:

Nails, Fishhooks, Blades, and Pebbles— You Won't Believe Your Eyes!

It's not a desk job. If it was, I'd get paper cuts.
When you walk down the street, you will stub
your toe, so you learn to watch how you walk.
—Harley Newman, sideshow performer

When I was younger, one of the television shows that end-lessly captivated me was *Kung Fu* starring David Carradine and Keye Luke. The way in which a hard-boiled kung fu flick was interwoven into the backdrop of the American Old West cap-tured my imagination in much the same way as Stephen King's gunslinger, Roland Deschain, did, roaming about a world right out of Tolkien's imagination. The two seemed like they would clash, but for some reason they worked and worked all too well.

And while I loved David Carradine's Kwai Chang Caine and the adventures he'd stumble on from week to week, what was more compulsively watchable to me were the flashbacks that involved a younger Caine and his blind mentor, Master Po, played with both finesse and ferocity by the skilled Keye Luke.

His character's mantra "Snatch the pebble from my hand, Grasshopper" has found its way into the pop culture consciousness. It both easily and quickly defines the relationship between mentor and student and the goal each has of attaining perfection in whatever it is that is to be learned.

All of this, particularly the centered, thoughtful, and ever-seeking perfectionist Master Po, was conjured in my mind when I first met Harley Newman. Newman's description of the way in which he would train for tightrope walking reinforced the image even more. Newman stretched a tightrope across his living room and made his way across the rope regularly. After a bit, he started to challenge himself, first by allowing his cat to sit on his head; then, later, he allowed his dog to climb onto his back. Cat on head, dog on back, all the while he focused on the movement of his feet across the rope, allowing himself to gain perfection in this one act. This is Master Po. This is Harley Newman.

No, Newman is not blind or Asian or a Shaolin monk. But in addition to being a skilled sideshow performer, Newman also has the skill as a mentor and teacher to be an asset to any student seeking his guidance. But it didn't come easily or overnight. Newman began performing sideshow stunts around 1982. He referred to it as a love/hate relationship and considered it a vocation, not a job. It's a life he lives, and it's not set in the confines or your typical nine-to-five job.

A full-time performer with a B.A. in theater and M.Ed. in counseling, Newman also teaches, writes, directs, and acts as a thaumaturge for a variety of other people. In 1972 he started to perform professionally as a clown. At the time, it wasn't considered a realistic option by his parents, but they were used to their son being a dreamer and a contrary. Eventually, however, when they attended the circus, they realized how skilled their son was at being funny and not only accepted his career choice but embraced it. "They finally realized that

I wasn't just a weird kid, but had become an eccentric adult. By the time I started doing stunts, they saw it as just other odd things in my repertoire."

In 1976 or 1977, Harley worked for Hoxie Tucker, who owned Hoxie Bros. Circus. There he wore many hats and worked on a lot of public relations-related things as well as clowning. While with Hoxie Bros., he lived in a trailer with some of the sideshow performers and did some of the outside talking and ticket sales for the sideshow. In the show, the Baron (Bill Unks) was the sword-swallower and fire-eater; Princess Margaret Ann (Robinson) was the little person; Joe Eddy (Fairchild) was the magician; and Marina Boyd, the wife of the sideshow manager, did the electric chair act and blade box. During his time with them, he learned a lot about the stunts and about training for them, so much so that he wasn't interested in actually performing them.

Eventually, by 1982, he'd learned and began performing his first two sideshow stunts, bed of nails and fire-eating, seeing it initially as a wise business decision that allowed him to diversify his performing abilities. And "not wanting to go back to clowning and the veritably low pay, seemed like a wise move."

He slowly expanded his repertoire over the years. In a regular show today he eats fire, stops a fan with his tongue, jams a high-heeled shoe or a power drill or both into his nose, staples his tongue to a board, swallows swords, walks barefoot on a ladder of swords, escapes from a straitjacket while riding a unicycle around the audience, hangs things from his eyes with fishhooks, and lies on a bed of nails.

As the instructor often pointed out during Sideshow School, presentation was everything, and this was something Newman took to heart. While his repertoire is far more extensive, he needs to find a good reason to put a stunt on stage. There must be the right story to frame it. And since he uses a lot of audience participation, he also needs to be very particular about how he gives directions to those participants.

"For a couple of stunts," he said, "if I mess up the directions, I'm going to get hurt, potentially fatally."

But with Newman everything was relative. While he hadn't required hospitalization for any of the stunts he performed, he had ripped an eyelid with a fishhook, had cracked ribs repeatedly, and had gotten regular abrasions and burns and pulled muscles.

"It's not a desk job. If it was, I'd get paper cuts. When you walk down the street you will stub your toe, so you learn to watch how you walk."

In creating a routine for any stunt, Harley seeks to do more than just entertain his audience, though he realizes that's the first thing that they're there for. Yet, he also seeks to astound and challenge them, hoping to make them aware that there may be other views of the world than the ones they habitually see.

"There is no such thing as a performance that isn't somewhat autobiographical. I love finding stories, what motivates people to move from one place to another, both physically and in their heads. This is the story of people. I'm an information junkie and often make connections that other folks might not see, or know about." Performing gives Newman a chance to share this with his audience.

"For example, the first recorded astronomical event was a comet, in 2357 B.C. Most people don't know of it. But there were devastating subsequent meteor impacts, widespread fires, earthquakes, rivers changing course and disappearing, and seas going wild. Fertile places were turned into desert. Cloud cover for the nine years following ruined agriculture in the Middle East, meaning that a lot of people starved to death and several of the most advanced cultures fell apart. When survivors migrated to places that weren't devastated, their philoso-

phy/religion changed. It shaped the modern world. It also pro-
foundly influenced stunt performance. I can talk about that,
give an idea of the depth of a stunt, then take it out of the
realm of 'lookit me, lookit me' and into a wider world of
human experience."

After almost every show Newman gives audience members
a unique opportunity to lie on a bed of nails. He's done this
over the last twenty-five years, giving a lot of people a different way to look at their fears. "I've heard regular stories
about how that's made a difference in someone's life, and it's
nice to know I've made a difference in the world."

In addition to being a sideshow performer, mentor, and
sideshow stunt guru, Newman has also done his part in coming up with original presentations of classic stunts. As *Sideshow
Gathering* had taught me, there's always something new to be
done with different stunts, and the way something is presented
is only hemmed in by the performers' imagination. This is
true of Newman and how he approached the bed of nails.

In 1982, when he first started doing the bed of nails, he
saw a one-paragraph article in *Circus Report* that mentioned
a performer who was going to try for the record for mini-
mum number of nails, using 11 nails. Unfortunately, the article didn't give any other information. It didn't say who was
going to do it or where they were going to do it. Ultimately,
the author never followed up with whether it happened.

The article began to bother Newman. He began to consider the 11 hypothetical nails, thinking about their placement,
and couldn't figure out where the 11th nail would go. Eventually, however, he figured out how to do 10, then 8, then 4.
A 4-nail bed of nails—science and David Blaine be damned,
this was a true feat of endurance!

He took the stunt, literally, to the American editor of the
Guiness Book of World Records, and performed it for him in his
office. Weeks later he received a rejection letter, stating that
while Harley was a highly trained professional, Guiness didn't

want people trying to emulate such a dangerous stunt. In true sideshow fashion, the fact that he wasn't included in the records books didn't bother Newman, being a reject was even more appealing.

However, he didn't stop there. In the late 1990s, Newman began doing a 2-nail bed of nails, but never came up with a proper way of presenting it that he liked, so he never performed it. Then, around 2001, he did 1 nail. A 1-nail bed of nails.

"It stayed on the back burner until '06, because it took that long to figure out the presentation and how to give directions to the people I ask to help." He's been performing the 1-nail bed of nails ever since. "Whether I keep it in my show is open to question. I have phantom sensations after performing the stunt. Initially, they'd disappear after about three days. Now it's a couple of weeks. I'm rather concerned about tissue degradation. It's a very intense stunt. I slipped once, and it took over a month for the wound to heal."

Not surprisingly, one of Newman's favorite stories to tell during a performance is that of Giles Corey. In 1692, eighty-year-old Giles Corey was accused of being a witch. He knew that by pleading guilty or not guilty, the state, as represented by the sheriff, George Corwin, would confiscate his property. So he didn't plead anything, which meant he couldn't be convicted. The penalty for refusing to plead, which had technically been outlawed twenty years earlier, was pressing. So on the appointed day, they led Corey onto the commons, stripped him naked, and tied him spread-eagle to stakes in the ground faceup. They put boards over him, and then piled on rocks. He refused to plead.

The next day, the sheriff asked him if he was ready to plead, and Corey said, "More weight." They added more rocks, asked if he was ready to plead, and his only response was "More weight." They continued to add weight until, ultimately, Corey died. His sons-in-law received his farm, not the sheriff. A number of years later, the sheriff was convicted of misusing his office for personal profit and ordered to return all the land and goods he'd stolen. He didn't.

"When he died," Newman said, "Corwin was buried in his basement, because the family knew that if he went into the churchyard his grave would be desecrated."

Newman couples this story with his bed-of-nail exploits. In addition to lying on four- and single-nail beds of nails, Newman also lies on traditional beds of nails with numerous people standing on various parts of his body. More weight? His personal best, thus far, has been holding 2,700 pounds of weight on his body while lying on a bed of nails.

"Now, that wasn't just people. It was a couple of ramps, a 900-plus-pound Harley Davidson, 500 pounds of riders and many more people. My nearest competitor for a stunt like this is 400 pounds less, and that performer passed out during the stunt."

With an eye on presentation and a desire to teach, all that's needed is a student willing to snatch the pebble from his hand.

CHAPTER SIX

∽◆

SIDESHOW SCHOOL, DAY THREE: A PYROMANIAC'S DELIGHT,

or, No, *Really*, How Stupid Do You Think I Am?

Fire bad!
> —Boris Karloff, The Monster, *Frankenstein*

No, no. Fire is good. Fire is good, yes! Fire is our friend.
> —Gene Hackman, Blindman,
> *Young Frankenstein*

Fire baaaaaaad!
> —Phil Hartman, Frankenstein,
> *Saturday Night Live*

Ever since man stood upright and made his way out of the cave in which he lived, turning his eye to the larger, colder world around him, he has sought to create and master fire. Such was the power of fire that once Prometheus stole the sacred element from the gods and bestowed it on man, he was forced to pay for his sin for all eternity. Tied to a rock, each day Prometheus was to have his kidney ripped out of his body and eaten by an eagle. Each night the kidney would grow back only to have the entire experience repeated again the next day. This was the price he paid for bringing fire to man.

Yet, master it we have. Fire-eaters and manipulators date back thousands of years, surely with performers entertaining Pharaohs in ancient Egypt. Today fire festivals and other performance art venues such as the annual Burning Man find performers displaying their love for, and their adept ability to manipulate and entertain with, fire. This then begs the question: If it's such an ancient art, and if it's so widely practiced today, then why is it that when I first attempted to learn it from a friend I nearly set my head on fire?

Okay, let's backtrack. This was probably around 1996 or so, long before Sideshow School and at a time when I was just rediscovering my love of magic. I'd gotten to know one of the salesmen at the local magic shop, and he mentioned in passing that he knew how to eat fire. I was intrigued.

Since the shop was quiet that day, we went into a nearby hall, with a torch, lighter, and bottle of lighter fluid in hand. He handed me the lighter, took the torch in hand, filled his mouth with lighter fluid, and jammed the bottle into his back pocket. I began to wonder what the fire marshall would think of all this had he known what was going on. We were in a fairly old building in Manhattan—a tinderbox, the walls peeling paint, the floors splintered wood, the drop ceiling missing tiles here and there. He motioned to me with one hand, his cheeks filled with the fluid like a chipmunk loaded with nuts.

"What?" I shrugged.

He motioned again.

"What?" I shrugged once more.

His eyes bulged and pointed at the lighter, his eyes now bulging in their sockets.

What can I say? He may have been a halfway decent magician, but his skills as a mime were for shit. He held the torch at arm's length from his body. I stepped forward, lit the torch with the lighter, then moved back. Way back. He took a deep

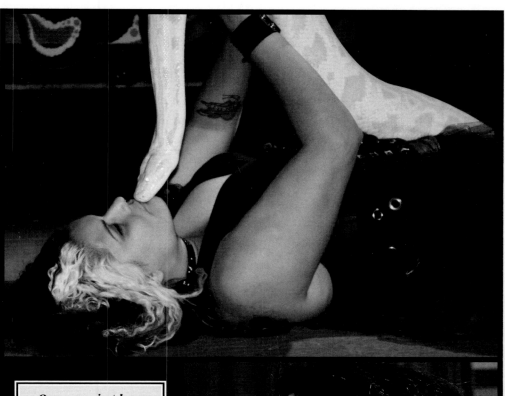

...Or are you just happy to see me? Snake charming with Serpentina of the Coney Island Circus Sideshow.

Ice scream.
Brett Loudermilk uses an icepick to hammer a nail into his nose.

Nipples of iron. The Great Nippo-lini lifts a fifty-five-pound anvil.

Postnasal drip. Through the nasopharynx and into the oropharynx, Todd Robbins has more fun with a balloon than most clowns.

Heartburn. Roderick Russell blasts a fireball into the air directly above his head. *(Courtesy Eric Tetreault)*

Tongue-lashing. Record-holder Gwyd the Unusual snaps a mousetrap onto his tongue. And without the benefit of cheese.

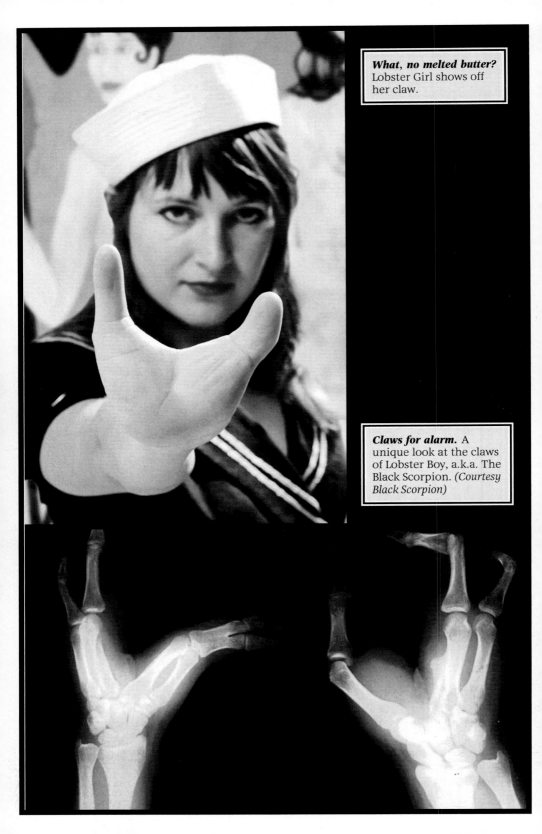

What, no melted butter? Lobster Girl shows off her claw.

Claws for alarm. A unique look at the claws of Lobster Boy, a.k.a. The Black Scorpion. *(Courtesy Black Scorpion)*

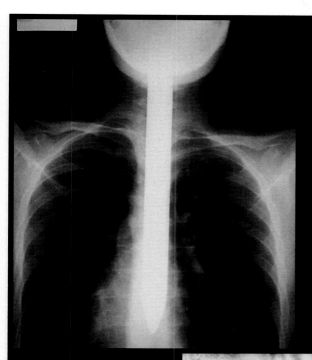

Heavy metal. An inside view of Roderick Russell's chest with a blade in place. *(Courtesy Dr. Eric Daly/CNY Medical Center)*

I am not an animal. I am a...something. Elephant Man strikes a startling pose. *(Courtesy Roj Rodriguez)*

Deep Throat. Damien Blade with a sword down his gullet.

Neon—it's what's for dinner. Queen of swords Natasha Veruschka prepares to swallow an emerald green sword crafted of neon.

Regina Slims. Reggie Bugmunch sucks in her stomach in order to pass her body through a tennis racket.

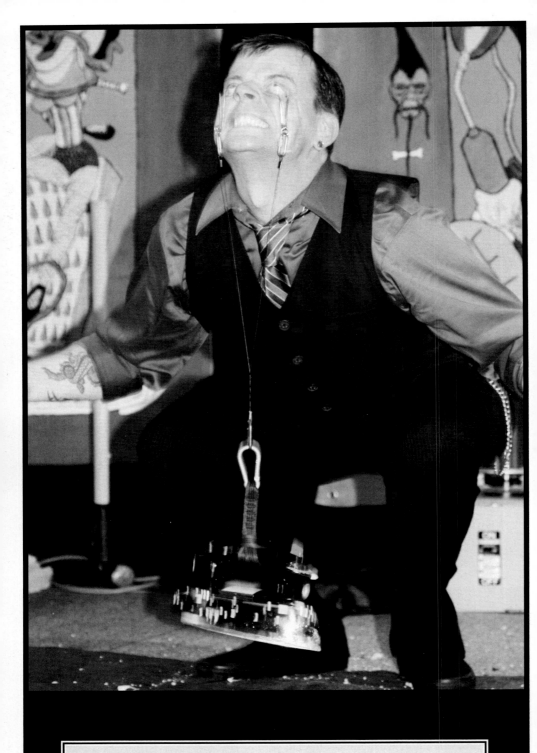

Don't try this at home, kids...oh, go ahead. Martin Ling the Suicide King lifts an iron connected to fish hooks hanging from his eyes.

breath through his nose and spewed the liquid forth, sending it on a one-way path to the torch, where it ignited in midair. Suddenly, the entire hallway was alight, as a brilliant fireball blazed. It churned its way up the length of the hall in the same way the explosion made its way up the elevator shaft toward John McClane in the original *Die Hard*. Yet, one second you could roast marshmallows in the hall; next, the event was completely over.

Then the door at the end of the hall opened and a young woman came out with a clipboard, completely oblivious. Had she come through the door five seconds earlier it would have been a completely different scene. By the time it was over, someone would have been dialing 911. But I took the stunt as proof that he was a professional, and weeks later, we holed up in his apartment where he taught me the fundamentals of eating and breathing fire. He was kind enough to lend me his torches with which to practice.

I took them home and mentioned what I was doing to my friend Tom. He had the wisdom of once pointing out to me that all former altar boys were reformed pyromaniacs, which I've come to believe is true. A secret lover of fire himself, we convened on the driveway behind his mother's home in Queens where I showed him what I'd learned. We dipped flaming torches into and out of our mouths, extinguishing them by cutting off the flames' oxygen by shutting our traps. The lack of oxygen and the confines of our saliva-dripping mouths would suffocate the flames instantly. We considered ourselves so badass. Of course, we didn't know enough then to close our teeth around the torch, rather than our lips, leaving me, at least, with some minor burns. But like Prometheus, there's always a price to be paid.

Tom asked about breathing fire, and I explained how difficult it was. My inside man at the magic shop had taught me that to do it properly we needed to be able to spray the lighter fluid from our mouths in one long burst. The ability to cut it off immediately being essential. We practiced using cups of water, spraying it out into the air from our puffed cheeks. After a while we were getting better at it, but we weren't confident enough to breathe fire just yet, so we put it off for another day; one that never came around for one reason or another.

This was a good thing, since the way I'd learned to eat fire, and the instruction I'd had about breathing fire, was 95 percent completely wrong. Had we tried breathing fire that day, I'm convinced one or both of us would have ended up in the hospital. Looking back, I recall us ending our session that day, our faces glistening from the water we'd spewed, our shirts nearly soaked. Had those spots on our skin and shirts been lighter fluid rather than water, we would have found ourselves on fire, flailing about on the ground like some sickening YouTube video. We'd have been *lucky* to walk away with second-degree burns.

Prior to attending Sideshow School, I'd heard all the myths and legends that most laypeople bandy about regarding fire-eating. Mostly, such beliefs lie in the fact that there's actually no such thing as fire-eating at all, that fire-eaters utilize a secret elixir called "cold fire" which is harmless but makes it look like the performer is actually eating fire. Nothing could be further from the truth. Fire-eating and fire breathing is just that. You're eating and breathing fire. It's dangerous, and, if not respected, can burn you. Unless you're playing with fire in the sacristy of a church in the middle of a mass, then it's okay. Alright, maybe not. But it is fun.

True to Tom's belief, some of my first experiences with fire prior to my faux classes with my friend from the magic shop were all in my youth, when boys will be boys and boys who are altar boys love fire. I clearly recall being part of a funeral mass and watching a fire get out of control in one of the rooms to the side of the altar. Altar boys use extremely long wicks, up to three feet long, to light the candles that are out of reach. During the funeral mass in question, one of my friends stepped off the altar and out of boredom began playing with one of the wicks, lighting it and putting it out, all out of the priest's sight line. Then the wick got out of control.

Before I knew it, my friend was stamping it out as quickly as he could, but was unable to completely defuse the situation. He motioned to me. Containing my laughter and trying hard to respect the grieving family, I calmly made my way off the altar, and the two of us furiously stamped out the mounting blaze with our feet. Thankfully, it was out before our robes caught on fire.

Let's go back a bit further. I'm home "sick" from school one day, and finding nothing but soap operas on television, decided to write my name on the tiled kitchen floor with a can of Lysol. I'm not sure if this is true now, but back then, Lysol was as flammable as a blowtorch.

After I'd written my name across the floor in big, two- to three-foot-high letters, I struck a match and watched as my name lit up the kitchen in brilliantly blue and orange flames. Seriously, it's a wonder I didn't burn down the house. We'll skip over the story where I cut an electrical wire with a pair of metal scissors, sending sparks flying in the then darkened room. That anecdote really doesn't apply here.

Okay, one final step backward. I was in fourth or fifth grade, and it was fall. I was over a friend's house, his parents nowhere to be found, and we brought an old coffee can onto his back porch. We dropped leaf after leaf into the can, setting them on fire one at a time. Then we made a mistake and dropped a lit match to the ground. His yard was filled with trees, and the grass completely covered with dried, dead leaves. Cue the slow motion of the match dropping to the ground. Cut to my friend and I watching it fall, our mouths hanging open aghast. Cut back to the match as it contacts that first leaf and sets it afire in an instant. Stop the slow motion and back to real time as the fire begins to consume not just the first leaf, but the one next to it and the one next to that. Suddenly it's like a wave of fire making its way through the yard. The fire spreads quickly, too quickly for us to manage, and before we know it, the entire yard is ablaze, tendrils of smoke rising, flames licking this way and that along the length of the yard.

One of us thinks to get the hose. I wish I could remember who it was, and, most of all, I wish I could say with some certainty it was me. But I'm sure it wasn't. I'm sure I was too in awe of the fire. So maybe I'm a closet pyromaniac. Or was. Who knows? But the thought of controlling fire intrigued me. The thought of eating fire turned me on. The thought of breathing fire brought me to damn near a climax. So let's start again. There is no such thing as cold fire. There is only fire. Hot, burning, dangerous fire, and in Sideshow School, we learned the fundamentals of eating it, manipulating it, and breathing it—*correctly*.

When our instructor gathered us in the sideshow theater to begin our work with fire, I'm reminded of the Bill Murray and Richard Dreyfuss film *What About Bob?* in which Dreyfuss's character, a psychiatrist, has come up with a new way of dealing with everyday phobias. The process is called baby stepping, and that's what learning to eat, manipulate, and breathe or blow fire is all about. It's about baby stepping. Taking one small, tiny step at a time. You don't just leap in; you have to start small, building and layering what you've learned. You can't just turn around and start spitting fire, otherwise you're liable to get hurt.

So where do we start exactly? We start with the torch. We're taught to make our first torches with which we'll learn. We're in the theater, some of us sitting on the bleachers where the audience would sit, and others are on the perimeter as our instructor shows us how to make a crude but workable torch using a wire hanger and some cotton cloth. Cotton is best because any other material, such as a polyester blend could feasibly burn out of your control, causing pieces of it possibly to melt and fall apart. Bits of flaming, hot, melting materials are the last things you want dropping into your mouth.

After we've each made our own torches, we gather in a circle. At the beginning of the week, I'd mentioned that I'd done some fire-eating in the past, so our instructor turns to me first. Whenever we're starting something new, we do it slowly, one person at a time, so that not only can the instructor focus on that one student should something go wrong, but the other students can also learn from the mistakes made by the rest of the students.

The directions are this: First, I'm supposed to dip the torch into the fluid. Second, I'm to shake off the excess, not wanting flaming fluid dripping into my mouth either. And third, I'm to tilt my head back slightly, open my mouth, insert the torch, and close my mouth around it, being sure not to bring my lips together, but, rather, sealing off the torch with my teeth.

Very little science goes into eating fire. Hot air rises. We know this from cold winters and the way in which second floors of many homes are warmer than the first floor. Alternatively, you can use hot air balloons as another good example. They use fire to fill the balloon with hot air, which in turn causes the balloon to rise from the ground. In addition, if you think about any flame, it licks upward. The heat and hot air are rising.

Next is oxygen. That's what allows any flame to live. Fire consumes and lives because of two things: oxygen and material to burn (fuel). Take any one of those two things away, and the flame will be extinguished.

When you're eating fire, when you're taking a flaming hot torch and tipping it into your mouth, there's one important thing to remember: don't inhale. You can hold your breath, and you can even exhale, but inhalation during the eating of fire is bad. Why? Well, think about this: fire lives on oxygen. It will go wherever it finds oxygen. So if you put the torch in your mouth, the flame is now in a situation where there's less oxygen—which is why the flames will lick upward out of your mouth.

However, if you make the mistake of inhaling, you'll be pulling oxygen into your lungs. The flames will follow the path of said oxygen, and, in the end, could seriously burn your lungs. That's right, you could burn your lungs. Consider this the next time you see fire-eaters plying their trade, and be sure to either throw them a tip or pat them on the back after their performance. They're treading a very dangerous line, all for your entertainment!

Now when it comes to the torch, what we're dealing with is a metal rod on which is a small cloth head. What happens when the flammable liquid on the cloth starts to burn is that the rod starts to get very hot. Therefore, it's important to make sure you close your teeth around it and not your lips. If you were to close your lips around it, they'd come in contact with the metal rod of your torch, which is very hot and will burn you. It will burn you. Yes, this is real fire. Again, this is dangerous. And again, do not take this as instruction! If you want to learn fire-eating, seek out a mentor.

So I listen to the directions, and I dip my torch into the fluid. I've done this before, and part of me is excited about doing it again after all these years—this time correctly. I shake off the excess and light my torch. It burns beautifully, blue, orange, and yellow dancing at the end of the rod, the head of the torch visible through the flame. I tilt my head back, bring the torch up above my head, then arc it downward toward my mouth.

That's when I realize that eating fire is nothing, absolutely nothing, like riding a bike. Just because you've done it before doesn't mean you can do it again. Time here is your enemy. Our bodies and minds are trained to know that, and Frankenstein would certainly agree, fire is bad. Even though you've done it before, it doesn't seem to matter. Your mind gets thrown into a sort of panic mode, and all you can think about is the ball of flame that your hand, conspirator that it is, is bringing directly toward your face.

I close my eyes, hoping the torch will enter, and start to close my mouth entirely too soon. Our instructor stops me and I extinguish the torch. I do so with a short sharp breath, like blowing out a giant birthday candle, and I'm led through the steps once more. I go through it all again, this time jazzed and knowing I'll do it. Dip. Light. Tilt head back. Bring torch up. Bring torch down. Insert torch in mouth.

Holy shit, that's a flaming torch near my face. I stop. This ain't happening. I mean, really. It's a flaming, fucking torch. They want me to put it in my mouth. *Really*, how stupid do you think I am? I turn to my other classmates who are watching, some curious, others anxious to get started themselves, still others worried that someone who apparently has done this before is having so much trouble. Maybe this is the act that'll break us all.

Our patient instructor goes through it all again. I attempt it again, and once more my brain goes into shut down. I can't do it. Six times this happens, and each time I'm either freezing up or attempting to close my mouth all too soon, long before the torch is fully in the confines of my mouth, meaning that I'd be closing my lips and teeth around the head of the torch, far from safe and sure to leave me with some serious burns. Finally, our teacher stands next to me and, like Christopher Walken in *Biloxi Blues,* begins to shout the commands as I go through the motions, telling me when to insert the torch into my mouth.

I bring the torch closer. Closer.

"IN, IN, IN...," he's shouting.

The torch gets closer.

"GO IN!"

I bring the torch closer.

"CLOSE YOUR TEETH, CLOSE THEM!"

I close my mouth, forgetting the teeth, and hear my lips sizzle a bit as they contact the hot rod of my torch. I'm burned, but the torch is extinguished. Sideshow School has just taught me to eat my first flaming torch.

I probe around momentarily in my mouth with my tongue. The oddest sensation about eating fire is the fact that your teeth and, in my case, any fillings you might have, get hot. My tongue contacts one of those fillings, and there's a slight hiss, a warmth emanating from them unlike anything either a hot drink or food can convey to your teeth.

As I turn, our instructor moves to the next student. He listens to the instruction, dips, lights, gets it in, and extinguishes his torch on the first try. God, I'm an asshole. Or is he? No, it's me.

It's not all that bad actually. Out of the group of us, we eat fire for the first time with varying success, some of us able to do it truly quickly; others are more hesitant about getting that first torch into our pie holes. We move on, working on getting the torch into our mouths with more confidence, and soon I'm able to do just that, though the moments when I'm required to extinguish the torch by closing my teeth is a frantic one more often than not. I continue to close my lips first rather than my teeth, and each time they're burned when they contact the rod of the torch.

It soon becomes an exercise similar to that of Pavlov's dog. How many times can you be burned before your brain finally takes in the fact that you need to close with your teeth and keep your lips apart in order to avoid the pain of a burn?

How many times? Too many to count. But soon I'm doing it, finally comfortable enough about getting the torch into my mouth. All fear of searing the mouth and tongue is set aside, so much so, that I can finally focus on the way in which I close my mouth, and the fact that, yes, if I do indeed seal off the torch with my teeth first, then the burns on my lips won't receive more burns. By the time we move on to the next phase of eating fire, the center of my upper and lower lips are red, sore, and tender.

We move on with each of us creating a second torch. The scene might best be described as a sort of kindergarten arts and crafts class as imagined by David Lynch. I think of the children in my son's preschool class and the way in which they slave over a coloring sheet or work tirelessly on cutting along the solid line on a piece of paper, their eyes focused, the tips of their tongues sticking out of the corner of their mouths. It's similar here, only we're sitting in a sideshow theater, some of us bending hangers in order to get the rod necessary for making the torch, others tearing cotton cloth for the head of the torch, and still others rolling the cloth around the end of the rod. Each of us seemingly in our own little world of creation until it's finally time to light the torches and attempt the next feat, which is a bit more complex.

The choreography of what we're about to do is explained and shown to us by our instructor: We'll first take our two torches, soak them in the liquid, and shake off all the excess. Next, we'll light one torch; touch the unlit torch with the tips of our fingers, thus getting a bit of the liquid on them; bring our fingers to the lit torch; allow our fingers to catch on fire; bring them back to contact the unlit torch, which will cause it to light; and then *casually* blow out our fingers. We're to follow all of this up by extinguishing both torches in our mouths. Thankfully, not at the same time.

We first run through the routine without actual fire, going through the motions and choreography because never having done this, it's a bit like patting your head and rubbing your tummy at the same time. You have to keep each step in mind, never hesitating for too long. Why? Because the longer you hesitate after a torch is lit, the longer it has to get hotter. And hotter. And hotter.

It was at this point that I thought how nice it would actually be if cold fire did exist. It would save us from all this worry of being burned and rushed to the hospital. Somewhere my younger, more pyromaniacal self chided me bitterly. Ridiculous, he seemed to say. Grow up and enjoy it!

Our instructor runs through the routine once more in real time with real fire, getting to the end and blowing out the fire on his fingers with all the casualness of James Bond removing a condom from his wallet. He's cool as a cucumber, so much so that it's surprising he even needs to put the two torches in his mouth to extinguish them. You'd almost expect them to flit out on their own under the pressure of his utter coolness. He's Fonzie of the sideshow, all he needed was the leather jacket. After he's finished, he turns to the class who, in turn one at a time, attempt to transfer the flame from one torch to another by way of their fingers.

We're far from casual, but we get the job done. When I attempt it, I get as far as lighting the second torch with my fingers. I'm so pleased with myself that I actually forget for a moment that my fingers are on fire and do the complete opposite of casual and begin shaking and blowing at them to put out the fire. I'm tempted to stop, drop, and roll, but the fire's so small and the floor so unaccommodating that I'd look foolish.

Though any attempts at not looking foolish were thrown out the window a few days earlier when I tossed the ice pick at the floor and hit my own foot. There's really no way around it. If you're going to forget that your hand is on fire and if upon realization that said hand is on fire you begin to flail about, there's nothing you can look like other than foolish.

I take a moment and thank god we're only transferring the fire using something innocuous as a finger. We could be using a completely different part of our body, something that might actually hurt a lot more if it were burned, like the tongue.

"Okay, let's try transferring the flame from one torch to another using our tongue."

Ah, our oh so cool instructor appears to not only channel

all the coolness of Arthur Fonzarelli, but also can read minds—
or is a sadist. Even by the end of Sideshow School I was never
sure which he was. Maybe both.

So, yes, the next step we take is transferring the flame from
one torch to another using our tongue as the conductor. Basically, we are slapping the tongue with the unlit torch to
allow a sufficient amount of flammable liquid to be left behind, then lighting the tongue with the other torch, and then
bringing the unlit torch to the flames dancing on the tongue.
No, REALLY, how stupid do you think I am?

During college I took a philosophy course in which there
were twenty students. The first week of the course we were in
a small room, each of us seated at a table with the professor at
the head. The next week, due to scheduling conflicts, we were
moved to a different, smaller room with a few less chairs. Some
of us sat on windowsills, others leaned against a wall. The week
after that we were moved yet again; this time we moved to an
even smaller room with even less chairs. The following week
the event happened again, but this time we were in a room
so small that it bordered on the comical. Someone offhandedly
suggested that there were cameras in all the rooms we'd been
in, and we were being watched by the psychology department
to see our reactions to being placed into smaller and smaller
rooms.

At no time during Sideshow School did I ever feel so much
like I was on some strange sort of reality show or on *Candid
Camera* as when we were told to transfer flames from one
torch to another using our tongues. In a lot of ways, it's a lot
like a good novel or a solid piece of fiction where the author
asks you to imbibe in the suspension of disbelief. You hear
the words you're being told and at first you don't believe
them, but then, after a bit, you go along with the gag.

In Sideshow School you're asked, slowly, to wade into the
waters. The first time you dip your toe into the water is a
chilling experience, and you're initially shocked. However, you

get used to it as you wade farther into the water. Then, suddenly, the shock comes back as you realize that you're now up to your neck in water that might very well be over your head very soon. The shock, the surprise, and the fear somehow sneak up on you again. And yet, somehow, you do it. It sounds insane. It sounds like it's the most off-kilter thing you've ever been asked to do, but you do it. And it's okay. I suppose that the hostages in Stockholm, Sweden, had similar feelings all those years ago.

But, in all seriousness, for some reason it's okay, and that's the moment, right then, when I lit my tongue on fire and used that lit tongue as a sort of makeshift lighter to bring the fire to the other torch. Yes, right then, I knew I could do pretty much anything. I'm sure whatever it was that I was attempting to do would take practice and time, but I'd just set my tongue on fire—*safely*. I was still breathing. I was still alive. What more was there to be afraid of? Not only had I learned to put fire out by enclosing it in my mouth, but I'd learned to light my tongue on fire. Really, how cool is that?

I soon came to realize that while it's alright and a perfectly human response to acknowledge the coolness and excitement of what you're doing, the adrenaline pumping through your body while you're doing something like this and the result of being successful at something such as lighting your tongue on fire can cause you to lose perspective and focus.

Tyler Fyre, fire performer (what else would he be with a name like "Fyre"), sword-swallower, and all-around sideshow geek of the *Lucky Daredevil Thrillshow* pointed out that "there are two times you can get hurt performing a dangerous act: In the beginning when you are learning a new act and don't have it perfected yet. And once you are so comfortable performing an act that you let your mind wander to other things. I have been lucky in over 10,000 live stage shows to have only a small handful of notable injuries."

True to this axiom, the next time I lit my tongue on fire,

still riding high from doing it correctly the first time, I nearly burned my cheek. With fire, more than anything else we'd dealt with in Sideshow School, your focus must always be on what you're doing every step of the way. If you're performing the Human Blockhead and you either push the nail in at the wrong angle or push it too deeply, you can bet your body will let you know that you're doing something wrong before you get too far. The discomfort and pain you feel will be a good indicator. But with fire, so much can go so wrong so quickly that you need to keep your wits about you every second and during every step.

A few years back, I attended a magic convention where a female magician performed a stage show using doves and some candles. She was performing a magic act, and at no point was the goal of the show to eat or manipulate fire. She simply had the candles onstage as a sort of decoration to enhance the mood. Yet, at one point, while she walked by the candles too closely, her hair caught on fire. The audience held its breath, unsure if this was part of the act or not, and within seconds a stagehand ran out to pat the flames out before they became out of control. The magician was oblivious to what was happening the entire time, consumed by what she needed to do next on stage.

So your focus and concentration can shift. Even for someone who wasn't even working with fire in the way a sideshow performer would it proved dangerous. Therefore, you need to consider the level of danger you're facing when you're actually seeking to work with and manipulate fire. Your concentration and focus on what you're doing needs to increase proportionately to the inherent danger of the act you're performing.

With that in mind, we step outside for a few attempts at fire breathing. It is the afternoon, and while it isn't raining, the day is overcast with a bit of a breeze driving its way down the street and a chill wind coming off the water a few blocks away. Not the optimal conditions for breathing fire, but it'll have to do.

Surprisingly, we train in much the same way as my friend Tom and I trained for the same stunt years earlier. We bring along bottles of water, and our first attempts are accomplished only using that. Our instructor takes a swig of water first and blows it out into the air to see which way the wind is blowing. Then standing in the center of the street, he takes a long draw from the appropriately flammable liquid, lights his torch, and breathes out a fireball the likes of which I'd never seen. The wind catches it, drawing it away from him as the air blazes.

The stunt catches the eye of a kid heading up the street toward the boardwalk. All kids, I've come to believe, are attracted to two things: fire and gum found on the ground. Given the right age, they'll either play with one or attempt to eat the other. The kid comes up to our instructor, eyes wide as pie plates, and asks if he can be next. Our instructor's *no* is terse, short, and direct, enough so that it conveys the message that the boy might very well want to put an egg in his shoe and beat it—which he does.

We begin with the water, filling our mouths and spitting it out into the air. The object here isn't just to spit the water but, rather, to turn your mouth into a kind of sprinkler system, infusing the liquid with as much air as you can as you blow it out so as to cause the droplets of liquid to be as tiny as possible. Should you be breathing a flammable liquid, the tinier the droplets are, the more massive and spread out your fireball will be.

We each give it a few tries with just water. The first breath gives us a chance to see exactly which way the wind is blowing, and most likely, each of us got a bit of water blown back into our faces on that first breath. But consider this: if we'd been using fuel rather than water, flames would've made their way back to us due to the wind.

Sideshow and Renaissance Fair performer Casey Severn,

known as Dash to his Ren fest audiences, considers blowing fireballs probably the most dangerous trick he's performed thus far. "I've set my face on fire. Twice. Once it was an outside event and the wind changed directions on me blowing the lit fuel back onto my face where I received minor second-degree burns and major first-degree burns. The second was in a nightclub on the stage, and as I blew out the fuel, the air conditioner kicked it back over my head. I received minor first-degree burns on my nose from that one. I don't do it anymore. I don't think I was meant to. Of course, if the money's right..." If the money's right most people will do *anything*.

After getting a gauge on which way the wind is blowing, we then attempt to blast a mouthful of water in such a way as to turn it not so much into water in the air but into a fine mist. Once we have that down, it's time to turn to fuel.

Needless to say, in addition to any dangers you might be running into of burning yourself alive, the additional danger to breathing fire is that you're putting a toxic substance in your mouth. There are those who might argue that you're spitting it back out, but trust me on this one, all of it *never* gets spat out. No matter how well you think you're spitting it out, blasting it into the perfect mist that you want it to be, without a doubt, you will swallow some of it. It's a risk you take.

And if you still don't believe me, then consider this: when you're eating fire and never actually filling your mouth with fluid, an hour or so later your stomach will roll a bit, you'll let out with a belch, and it will, most certainly, taste of the fuel you've been using on your torches. Again, here you're not even filling your mouth with the fluid, but you're still ingesting it to some degree.

Sensoriel, the fire performer that's part of the *Cheeky Monkey Sideshow* in Washington, DC, performs a truly magnificent act in which she weaves dancing with fire-eating, the entire routine culminating in a performance in which she makes use of two large fans composed of five lit torches each. As she spins and twirls about the stage, the fire dances also, lapping at her face and body, yet all the while in her control.

After the show, I asked her if she also breathes fire, and she noted that it was not something she did often. "When I eat fire, I'm already ingesting so much that's toxic that I don't see the need to do my body even more harm."

There's really no way around it. If you're going to be eating fire, if you're going to be breathing fire, then you're going to be putting toxic substances into your body. So the risks are twofold: you can run the risk of getting burned, and you can also run the risk of being poisoned—hazards of the job. Though fire workers do point out that you're ingesting minimal amounts of fuel during a performance, it must be noted that, nonetheless, it's minimal amounts of a *toxic* substance. I'm just putting that out there for your consideration. Think before you leap, even once you find a mentor.

Back to breathing fire. Once I evaluate the wind and spit a few test blasts, I fill my mouth with fuel. It's wretched, and you don't want to keep it in there very long. As I'm lighting the torch, preparing to let loose with my blast of fire, a thought crosses my mind that the revolting taste and feel of the fluid could easily be ended quickly if I just swallow it, but I'm sure that will make for a one-way trip to the hospital. I am almost three days into Sideshow School without having to call my wife from an emergency room.

It seems I am hedging my bets the longer I hold the fluid in my mouth. I hold up the torch, breathe deeply through my nose, and let loose with as large a blast as I can. The fireball is pathetic, but nonetheless there and visible. Miniscule yet glorious at the same time, it is there in front of me one second and gone the next, nothing more than vapors and the scent of the fuel hanging in the air.

I turn and spit any residual fuel left in my mouth on the ground. Then, when I return to the sidewalk to allow the next student a try, I turn to a trashcan and spit again—and again. It's a nasty taste, truly stomach churning, but I regret nothing. I have eaten fire. I have breathed fire as a dragon would breathe fire.

Somewhere Prometheus was paying for his sins yet again by having his kidney ripped from his body by the beak of an eagle. I couldn't have been happier.

CHAPTER SEVEN

THE FREAKOPHILES PRESENT THE STRANGE TALE OF TYLER FYRE & THRILL KILL JILL:

Love, Luck, and Fire-Eating—Alive on Stage!

It was a spectacular world I had never seen and could not get enough of.
—Tyler Fyre, *Lucky Daredevil Thrillshow*

It was then that I realized the audience is always waiting for the snake to bite me during the act.
—Thrill Kill Jill, *Lucky Daredevil Thrill Show*

Tyler Fyre and Thrill Kill Jill are the two performers who make up the *Lucky Daredevil Thrillshow*. A nearly seamless pairing onstage, they're partners together offstage as well, which is an interesting dynamic when you think about it. There are so many marriages comprised of couples who *don't* work together and end up in either separation or divorce, that the existence of the *Lucky Daredevil Thrillshow* almost begs the question: Exactly how long can two people stand to be around each other before one starts to consider setting the other on fire? Given the chemistry these two performers share onstage, you have to hope forever.

One of Tyler's earliest memories is of attending the *Ringling Bros. and Barnum & Bailey Circus* in Atlanta, Georgia. Still in possession of the original program from that show, his childhood memory is of the show being everything it promised to be, living up to the name "The Greatest Show on Earth." At the time Gunther Gable Williams was headlining, with his blond mane of hair and sequined costumes catching the spotlights, Williams climbed into cages to face hungry tigers, a smile ever on his face. "It was a spectacular world I had never seen and could not get enough of," Tyler said, recalling Williams' act giving way to the flying trapeze, the high wire, and bears riding motorcycles.

Around the same time, Tyler stumbled onto a book at his grandmother's house by James Otis titled *Toby Tyler or Ten Weeks with the Circus*. Later made into a Disney film, the book told the story of a young boy who ran away with the circus only to find the life much harder than he'd envisioned. The reality of his situation eventually drives the boy back home, the experience heightening his appreciation for his true family. But that wasn't what Tyler took away from the book. In fact, the book coupled with the experience of attending a circus show had the opposite effect.

"You could say I ran away to join the circus, found out how much work it was, and realized that I wouldn't have it any other way."

As a boy, Tyler's father was a preacher, and in many ways this eventually left an impression on him as a performer. "He has a great way of telling stories and reaching people when he talks," Tyler said, pointing to this as one of his great inspirations as a performer, the other being Evel Knievel, whose exploits he followed from a young age.

"I look up to Evel Knievel for his showmanship in creating spectacular stunts and a lasting legacy." A statement that says much about the thrill show he would later create.

From the age of eight, Tyler was constantly working, going

from paper routes to making pizza and then from building sets and props for Broadway plays to decorating the windows at Saks Fifth Avenue. It was while in college that a change came about.

"I took a circus class where I learned how to juggle, walk a tightrope, balance things, and other circus basics. I started hanging out with some friends from that class and learned how to eat fire. I loved it, and more than the acts, I liked the people in the world of the circus and the sideshow."

Tyler's first full-time gig was at an amusement park in North Carolina where he performed magic and juggling in association with a fire-eating routine he tacked on to the end.

"If you had seen me juggle or do magic, you'd be amazed that my career didn't end quickly right then." He admitted the fire-eating at that time was far from what it should have been as well, but he soon learned how to make it better. "Eating fire five shows a day outdoors by the lake with swirling winds paved the way for the act to get good later."

He eventually found his way to Coney Island where he started out as an outside talker, luring potential audience members into the show. "Frank Hartman was the fire-eater, among other things, in the show. When I saw his fire act, I realized I had a lot left to learn. And learn I did while on Coney Island. Lots of it was from Frank, but also from the countless other performers who worked there over the years and those who came to visit. Bobby Reynolds set up his *Believe It Your Nuts* sideshow tent across the midway from us, so it was me talking against Bobby talking. Even though we were competing on the same midway, he would come over and give me tips on talking the show. Ward Hall taught me about talking the front of a show too. Frank Hartman kept me from killing myself while I learned to swallow swords. Todd Robbins gave me tips and pointers about how to present acts of all kinds and how to make them my own."

Tyler worked in Coney Island and stayed with them for seven years.

"For the first three I worked as the outside talker on the show, some folks call this person the barker, he's the guy you see on the movies saying 'Step Right Up!' There's a little more to it, and it's a great job. I didn't really even want that job when I took it. I wanted to be a fire-eater in the show. Little did I know that it's much easier to learn to eat fire than it is to talk the front of a show. And let me tell you, I wasn't great when I started. But as the talker, I was onstage with a microphone and no props twelve hours a day getting people's attention in the middle of a crowded midway, entertaining them, and getting them not just to laugh and clap, but to reach into their wallets and buy a ticket.

"The experience I got on the bally stage on Coney Island paved the way for everything else. After that, I worked inside the show for four years as the inside lecturer, or MC, doing several of the working acts, introducing the other performers, and pitching the two dings (acts that make the show extra money): a blade box and the blowoff. So I got the applause and still got to see the people line up with a dollar in their hand. It was a great job—a hard job, but a great job. I left Coney Island to work under the Big Top of the *Brothers Grim Sideshow*, which has always had a great cast and it was a thrill to work with them. With them I got to travel again. Coney Island was a great show to work on, but it kept me in one place."

With the *Brothers Grim Sideshow*, Tyler received an even more realistic experience of circus work since everyone worked hard to bring all aspects of the show to fruition. Performers weren't just performers. "On *Brothers Grim* I pounded tent stakes, rolled canvas, tied down the tent in the rain, slept under the big top on nice summer nights, and talked the front of the show with a 100-foot banner line behind me. I've been lucky to learn the hard work behind the scenes on a traveling show."

Tyler continued performing until, in 2006, he met his future partner—both onstage and offstage—at the *Burlesque-A-Pades*.

"I used to work tattoo and horror conventions," Jill recalled, "with a guy named Andrew D. Gore and his company *Satan's Sideshow*. Andrew makes horror and true crime merchandise and then sells it online and at conventions. Through Andrew, I found out about the book *Shocked & Amazed* and started reading about the sideshow world past and present. Then I met James Taylor, author of *Shocked and Amazed* and former co-owner of the American Dime Museum in Baltimore, Maryland."

Taylor, it turned out, was involved in putting together a theater/performance space in Washington, DC, which would eventually go by the name of The Palace of Wonders, and in addition to a stage would also include a small museum that housed some of the more bizarre items from Taylor's collection. It was after meeting Taylor that Jill's help was enlisted. "Shortly thereafter, I started designing the Palace of Wonders in Washington, DC, which features a museum of oddities owned by James Taylor. I started designing the Palace in 2004 and completed it in 2006. I booked the shows there for a couple years, and I was at a local show, the *Burlesque-A-Pades*, on Valentine's Day 2006 talent scouting when I met Tyler Fyre. We fell in love, got married in Las Vegas by Elvis on Valentine's Day 2007, and started the show we have out on the road now, the *Lucky Daredevil Thrillshow*."

Prior to meeting Tyler, Jill had no experience performing sideshow stunts. "I fell in love with a sideshow performer and that's what made me want to perform. Now the show is a way for me to travel with my husband/best friend and get paid to do it!"

Much like her husband, Jill is multifaceted and performs many acts in the show, including sword-swallowing and the Ancient Egyptian Cabinet of Death. The Cabinet of Death is their version of the blade box routine where everyone shares in the secret and in the fun of the show for a small fee and leaves the stage having gotten an up-close view of a spec-

tacular show business secret, a bed-of-nails routine that includes the Chainsaw Picnic, where while lying on the bed of
nails her husband cuts a pumpkin on her chest with a chainsaw. She also acts as the show's snake charmer, from which
she received one of her more memorable injuries.

"I was attacked by one of my snakes, Taker, a nine-foot, sixty-
two-pound boa onstage once. Tyler and I were hosting the opening party of *Exotic World* in Las Vegas when Taker bit me in
the face. I immediately pulled her off my head and handed
her off to Tyler on the side of the stage and went back to finish the act. I then realized that my face was bleeding, so I
finished the act, without the snake of course, and cleaned up
offstage.

"The audience didn't miss a beat and immediately started
cheering. It was then that I realized the audience is always
waiting for the snake to bite me during that act. Realizing
that has helped me play into people's fears and imaginations
during the act, which has made it a much more memorable
and exotic moment in the show."

The *Lucky Daredevil Thrillshow* travels seven months out of
the year, going where the shows are and where audiences
want to be entertained. "We look up to entertainers like Elvis
Presley, Evel Knievel, and Liberace," Tyler says, "who were all
pushing the edge of entertainment but struck a chord with
all kinds of people across America and the world. So we've
themed our show and our presentation to be like a Las Vegas
review show that's edgy and exciting and appealing to a wide
variety of people."

Painstaking entertainers who are always looking for a new
or original angle for an act, in addition to the Chainsaw Picnic, they also perform one of the most amazing routines that
combines sword-swallowing and fire-breathing. In the grand
finale of their show, Tyler swallows a specially made sword
whose handle has been fashioned into a torch that can be
used for fire-eating. Wielding the lit sword on stage, the han-

dle blazing, Tyler slides the sword down into his throat, the flaming handle protruding from his mouth. It's at this point that Jill, her mouth filled with fuel, steps up and blasts the fluid at the lit torch, igniting a fireball in the air over both their heads. Much like the two performers displaying the feat, it's a showstopper.

≈⌐

CHAPTER EIGHT

SIDESHOW SCHOOL, DAY FOUR: BROKEN GLASS AND ANIMAL TRAPS,

or, Damn, That's *Got* to Hurt!

Sometimes glass glitters more than diamonds because it has more to prove.

—Terry Pratchett

Man is the only kind of varmint who sets his own trap, baits it, then steps on it.

—John Steinbeck

We've almost come to the end of Sideshow School, and on the fourth day I'm already feeling a bit of nostalgia for something that hasn't even come to an end. It's a feeling that I hadn't felt for some time; it's a feeling I'd equate to being a kid and coming to the realization that you're staring down the barrel of the last week of summer vacation. You're melancholy and want to squeeze the most out of every final minute, which is what many of us do, on this, our penultimate class of the week.

At the end of the prior day, our instructor offered to allow us to show up early and play with fire a bit before class starts.

I'm excited about this as I leave home. My family and I, at the time, lived in an apartment in Queens, New York. Finding a place to practice such a skill as fire-eating was a futile effort, therefore I packed up the torches I'd made, climbed in the car, and headed for the Belt Parkway that would bring me to Coney Island. On a good day, the ride would take no more than forty minutes or so. This was *not* a good day.

Traffic turned an at most forty-five-minute ride into nearly two hours. My frustration level kept rising as the cars in front of me crawled along, ultimately spilling us out at a spot where two lone workmen had closed down one lane, seemingly so they could sit and have their coffee and bagels. Ah, the infrastructure of New York, it's a well-oiled machine going nowhere.

I arrived with less than half an hour left before class started and found my classmates on the stage of the sideshow theater lighting torches and prodding them into their mouths, transferring flames via fingers and tongues, some even attempting another feat: to retain the flame in their mouths, which is what I'd planned to work on that morning. It's a tricky sort of stunt that takes some practice. Basically, you dip your torch into your mouth and remove it while pursing your lips a bit so that a flame can be seen flicking from your lips.

I found the fluid, dipped my torch in, and went to work, our instructor taking care of some business not far away, always with a watchful eye on us and we with watchful eyes on each other. I lit a torch, tipped my head back, inserted the torch, and removed it, puckering my lips slightly in the hopes of retaining the flame. The problem, of course, was being able to see if I actually did what I set out to do. With my head tipped back and much of my concentration on keeping a certain degree of vigilance about my torch, it was difficult to take the few extra moments to attempt to see if I had actually done what I set out to do.

"Try it again," our instructor called over to me.

"Try it like this," another classmate suggested, and I watched him go through the moves. He was smooth and quick about it, his control of the torch filled with confidence. He tipped his head back, inserted the torch, began to close his mouth around it, and removed the torch. The torch was held to his side, but from his mouth was a bright, beautiful flame, gently licking the air, flickering once, twice, and then gone.

I tried it again, this time I moved more slowly. It was my speed, you see. When you're dealing with fire, you're constantly attempting to overcome the desire to get the flame away from you as quickly as possible. The confidence that you won't be burned if you do it correctly is thrown by the wayside, and all you want to do is get it in and out as quickly as possible.

But in an attempt to reach my personal goal of retaining the flame in my mouth that morning, I forced myself to slow down, inserting the torch, removing it, and—nothing.

"Slower," my instructor says, "and focus on the way in which you hold your mouth and lips as you remove the torch."

I did it again, and again, and again. I was convinced I wouldn't be able to get it, but I tried it a last time. And as my head tipped back, my eyes on the ceiling above, I heard one of my classmates exclaim, "Nice!"

I looked over and he's nodding. I turn to my instructor who was nodding. "Now," he says, "you are a man."

If only I'd been able to see it. If only I'd known. But I relished the moment nonetheless, took the flaming torch, inserted it into my mouth to extinguish it, and completely forgot to close my teeth around it first, and, instead, brought my lips closed, which contacted the rod of the torch—burns on top of burns. I'd gotten used to it.

As our instructor came over to the stage area, we put our torches away, sealed up the flammable fluid, and got ready for the day's lessons.

As a magician and performer, you're always looking for the perfect routine that you can bring with you and perform almost anywhere. The phrase that's most often used is "Packs small, plays big." That's one of the keys to any entertaining routine. You want something that packs small and is easy to carry, but by the same token, it must be something that'll play huge for the audience and be highly entertaining.

During the week of Sideshow School, I kept this mantra in mind. I wasn't exactly sure how I would ultimately use the skills I was learning, that was something I'd consider later on after I'd put in more hours of practice—much more than the time Sideshow School was allowing me. Sure, you're learning the acts, coming to understand the skills, but that's not enough. You need to put practice time into what you've learned. And once you have got that down, then comes the even more difficult task of making those skills entertaining, framing them in a manner that's appealing to an audience.

So, at the very least, as we learned each skill, I took into consideration whether it was something that packed small and played big. Certainly, the Blockhead was something that fit this bill, as Melvin Burkhart and Todd Robbins can attest with their unique presentations that they honed and fleshed out to create full-blown routines. The potential for the human blockhead is great, and it certainly packs small. Very small.

The bed of nails, on the other hand, was the complete opposite. It may play big with the right presentation such as Tyler Fyre and Thrill Kill Jill's Chainsaw Picnic, but the bed of nails itself was large, cumbersome, and heavy. It wasn't something that you would want to drag around from show to show along with the myriad of other items you might bring with you.

So that's the spectrum. You've an act as small as the human blockhead and as large as the bed of nails. Ideally, things that fall closer to the blockhead on the spectrum are items that can be easily transported, and that's what I was looking for. So I was pleased when our instructor walked forward on the stage with only a metal pail.

In the pail was a large piece of canvas, which he removed,

and laid out on the floor. Then he dumped the contents of the pail onto the canvas, a mass of broken glass tinkering and clattering.

"One of the things we'll do today," our instructor tells us, "is walk on glass."

He sits on the edge of the stage and removes his shoes and socks, then requests that one of us examine his feet, which we do, finding no signs of any protection. He then makes his way to the broken glass. He makes note of several nasty looking shards, and even holds up the broken neck and a shattered base, from which extend stalagmites and stalactites of glass that come to points as sharp as knives. He adds these back to the pile and stands with the glass in front of him, then gingerly steps onto the glass. Crunching sounds pervade the theater as glass grinds against glass under his weight. Then he asks one of us to pick a number between one and ten. Someone calls out the number seven, and he immediately begins to jump on the pile of glass—*seven times*.

Stepping off the glass he gives us the opportunity to examine his feet once more. When I look, I fully expect to see a bloody, pulpy mass of flesh, but instead, I simply see two feet made for walking—not a cut or a scratch can be found.

I'm fascinated, not only with the effect itself, but also because of it falling within the packs small and plays big spectrum. The props aren't so bulky as to allow me to rule them out as useful. All you have is a pail, a piece of canvas, and some broken glass. The rest is up to the performer to infuse it with his or her personality and routine to make it entertaining.

It's our turn to try it, and while I'm fascinated by the act itself and the potential behind it, standing to the side and watching my classmates remove their shoes, what it is we're doing suddenly strikes me. We're walking on broken glass, and the image that I'd fully expected to find on the bottom of our instructor's feet fills my head: a pair of bloody, pulpy feet. As with every other day I'd spent at Sideshow School, I find it hardly surprising and almost expected that there's hesitation, not only by myself, but by others in what we're doing. Even though we'd just seen someone do it, there's still an underlying belief that maybe it was a trick and that we didn't yet know the secret.

This belief is partially true. Really, there is no secret, but, rather, a variety of scientific principles similar to the ones that allow someone to lie on a bed of nails. Rather than nails, you have a pile of broken glass. Now going back to the bed-of-nails theory, if you were barefoot and you attempted to stand on a bed of nails consisting of, say, one nail (fool that you are), that nail would pierce your foot, impaling it instantly. However, if you were to increase the number of nails, the weight that your foot is bearing is spread out over those nails, making it easier to stand on.

The same goes for broken glass. But there are differences. With the glass, you don't have the luxury of having a consistent and even layer of nails. The glass at your feet is in a chaotic pile, with sharp edges pointing this way and that, some pieces stacked on others, and the potential for a shard of glass to suddenly slide out from beneath another piece of glass is always at the forefront. So care must be taken.

With the bed of nails, once you're comfortably lying down on it, the work, for the most part, is already done. However, with a pile of glass you always have to be on your guard. Once your feet are in place, once you've found a way to stand that doesn't involve a sharp edge digging into the soles of your feet, you've got to remain aware that should you shift your feet even the smallest amount, the opportunity for a different piece of glass to come into play is always there. So a *lot* of care must be taken.

One by one we make our way to the pile, and one by one we step onto the glass. As a child, my family went to the Jersey shore every summer, and as I grew older and the trips ceased, I'd often go down and visit my sister, who lived on the Jersey shore for a time. I'd spend a few weeks at her apartment during the summer, which was just blocks from the beach.

Now, I've never actually been much of a beach person and truly preferred the pool to the ocean or a lake. And if that pool's heated, more power to it! But I always enjoyed walking along the beach and finding shells, making sand castles, and digging holes,—which is what I did on the beach as a child, and I still do as an adult.

For the most part, the beaches were beautiful. But I recall one summer when I was young, just prior to the summer rolling in, the city had come to the realization that the beach was eroding away a bit. Someone came up with the bright idea of dredging sand from the bottom of either the ocean or the bay and pumping the wet mass onto the area of the beach that was eroding, thus replacing the sand there. To someone, it must have seemed like a good idea.

But I recall going down to the beach that summer and finding an unusual strip of land ranging from the road to the ocean. First, there was a strip of immaculate white sand, then a strip of shells, and then another strip of beach, this one gray and even thicker with shells.

Now I'm not talking just a few shells. I'm talking thousands— probably millions. And in these strips of beach filled with shells, literally no place existed where you could put your foot and not come down on a seashell.

Not only that, but these weren't the perfect shells that you'd go to the beach and collect. Whether it was because they'd been dredged from the bottom of some ungodly landfill or because it was the result of the actual dredging process, the shells were all broken. Very few shells were actually intact.

So you had this wide strip of land that was completely composed of broken shells. Were you of the mind to head down for a swim, the walk down to the ocean was a perilous one—unless, of course, you knew how to walk on broken glass—same situation.

Though I must admit, it's not something I thought of during Sideshow School when I was standing in front of that pile of glass readying myself to walk on it. But the situation really is very similar.

If you've ever been to the beach and encountered anything similar, you must know what it's like to either walk on broken shells or watch someone make their way across a path of broken shells. Their movements are quick, precarious, and careful—all at the same time.

It makes the person (me) walking across the broken shells look as if he's having some sort of full-body fit or episode, his muscles twitching and heaving as he takes one painful step after another. And yes, feel free to mock me. I was a kid and never considered the option of actually leaving my shoes on during this sojourn across the sharp and edgy oasis.

But looking back, those trips across the mass of broken shells were more painful than standing on, walking on, or jumping on a pile of broken glass. With the glass you have more control. Once you're standing on it, you can gently move your feet around and either roll any of the sharper pieces out of the way or turn them facedown; then once you've gotten yourself into a really good spot, you can jump up and down—several times.

Not that there isn't a risk of cutting yourself—there is. But if you're careful about where and how you're standing prior to jumping, you can walk away without being maimed—which when you see what some performers have done with a pile of glass would surprise you.

Stephon Walker, better known as Swami Yomahmi and part of the *Cheeky Monkey Sideshow* out of Washington, DC, first introduces his carpet of glass by breaking a fresh bottle into it before the audience—just in case anyone present was considering that he wasn't, in fact, using real glass. Then after making his way barefoot across the glass, he does a bit of a victory dance. Nothing too unusual, and certainly nothing that'd cause you to rummage in your pockets for singles to stuff into his pants, but it does add a much-needed moment of humor before he ratchets things up.

After finding himself a willing audience member, Walker drops himself to the floor, removes his glasses, and lays his unprotected face against the glass. The side of his face is clearly pressed against the chunks and shards of glass resting there. Then, to cap things off, he has the audience member step on his head, further pressing his face down. With the microphone by his head, you can audibly hear the crunching, grinding sound of the glass beneath the flesh of his face as the full weight of the spectator rests on his head.

If you think that sounds insane, then you haven't had the opportunity to see Martin Ling the Suicide King of the *Olde City Sideshow* out of Philadelphia. Prior to even walking on the glass, Ling hunkers down before the broken glass. Jagged edges and bottlenecks are clearly visible as he crouches as if before a babbling brook. He then brings his hands together and reaches down into the pile of glass. He fills them as he would if he were before a stream, preparing to wash his face with cool, clear water. Rather than water, though, he then proceeds to scrub his face with the broken glass, bringing them to his all too vulnerable forehead, eyes, nose, cheeks, lips, and chin. The glass showers over his face, the sound of it raining down to the floor nearly as disconcerting as the ensuing crunching sounds that followed Walker's face-to-the-floor stunt.

The unusual thing about Ling's exploit is that he *follows* the face washing with glass walking. At first it seems as if the glass walking would diminish the theatrical power of the entire routine since it gives the impression the face washing should come last being that it feels more harrowing. But that's hardly the case. With jagged edges and piercing, knife-quality shards protruding from the mass of glass, the anticipation and anxiety conjured up by the audience is only heightened by the sounds of Ling walking through the glass. You would almost expect there to be copious amounts of blood by the end, but there's not.

While it wasn't taught in Sideshow School, the leap between glass walking and fire walking is a short one. However, fire walking calls for a bit more timing, skill, and pacing as performer Roderick Russell pointed out to me. Neither the glass walking nor fire walking are without their risks though.

"Walking on fire or hot coals is a matter of confidence more than anything else," Russell explained. "That said, you can come through it completely unscathed if you have confidence and you walk with confidence, but that should not diminish the danger in your mind because I am proof positive that if you lack the confidence even a little bit, you can come through it with major injuries. I used to lead fire-walking groups, and I'd done it hundreds of times and led many groups across the coals, and I'm always the first one to walk, of course, to set the example, and show them that yes it can be done.

"But this one time, I tend the fire all day long. I'm the one who builds it, I'm the one who rakes it all out, and I have a penchant for long, wide, deep fire pits because they look really daunting, and I think it's a bigger psychological obstacle in people's minds than just a narrow strip of coals as you typically see. So I build them big for that psychological reason so they really feel like they're really accomplishing something rather than fooling themselves into thinking they did something cool.

"But here I am standing in front of these coals, and it was just two days after I had made a major relocation of my residence, had made a major change in my financial status and investments, and had just totaled my best friend and business partner's car in an accident. And not only was his vehicle totaled, but *I was in a car accident.* I had to deal with that too. And I had all these things weighing on my chest and on my mind, and I was standing there, in front of the pit, and I said to myself in my head 'You know, I'm probably going to burn myself this time.' And that's just the wrong thing to say to yourself before you walk on coals.

"I took the first step, and when I took that first step I knew, it just seared straight through my foot and I couldn't do anything about it. I just had to keep going. So I took the second step, and I felt that one too, and I knew I had to keep going. So I walked all the way to the end of the pit, and I turned and I gestured for everyone else to follow me. And everyone did. And everyone was perfectly fine, except for me.

"Now I couldn't let on that I was injured at all, because if I did, it would blow the experience for everyone, and probably more people would have been injured. But I had to stand there for a good hour between the walking, some people wanting to re-walk it, and then the chitchat and then the wrap-up and then seeing everyone off. I had to stand there for a good hour with third-degree burns on the bottom of my feet.

"I then got whisked away after the event to the place that I was staying and got my feet into a bathtub, where it became evident that this was *not* a bathtub injury. It was more like an *emergency room* injury. So we went to the emergency room, and I spent many hours there, and I had to follow that up with a burn clinic a few days later and with a return trip to the burn clinic the week after that. And I was off my feet, I was on crutches, and I was in a wheelchair for about a month solid.

"In the burn clinic, they had to take a scalpel and cut off all the dead skin and pull it back, and they exposed all the muscle underneath, and there it was very clear: white dead spots of muscle. It was a very bad injury.

"The most amazing thing though was sitting in the emergency room. I was sitting in a wheelchair at the registration desk, and I'm doing all I can to focus my mind on the pain so I can experience the pain and feel the pain so that it doesn't overwhelm me, because I'd never quite felt pain like that before. It was intense, and it was taking all of my concentration just to be with it and not let it overwhelm me. And my girlfriend at the time was rubbing my arm trying to be consoling, and gently saying 'It's going to be okay, you're going to be alright.' I actually had to ask her to stop rubbing my arm because it was dividing my attention so much that it was making the pain worse. And it was just such an interesting psychological moment to realize that dividing my attention could intensify the pain."

While injuries were limited to minor cuts, burns, and abrasions while at Sideshow School, once you begin performing such feats on a regular basis, the risk goes up. The more you do anything, the more of a chance you have to injure yourself. I'd walked on glass and fully expected to walk away with my feet cut to ribbons, but it can be done safely. Assuming you know what you're doing.

After a break for lunch, during which I find my way to Nathan's, scarf down a few hot dogs, and return back to the sideshow, I'm faced with a bright, shiny animal trap.

Small animal traps, the kind that are marketed for use on animals like raccoons, are extremely dangerous. They work off a powerful spring that causes the trap to slam shut. If you were to put your own foot in there, it probably wouldn't break your leg, but it'd certainly break the leg of a small animal, and it'd certainly break a finger or two if you were to go poking around in it without some sort of direction.

The nice part about small-spring animal traps is that they don't, traditionally, have teeth. In fact, looking at the mouth of the trap is a lot like looking into the mouth of a person who has removed his dentures.

Nice, of course, is relative here. Since we're in Sideshow School, everything's relative. Sure, it's nice that the trap doesn't have any teeth, but, by the same token, the spring is so powerful that if you place your hand in it the wrong way you could break a finger or two. So, yeah, the trap is nice—shiny too. Since traps like these are rarely used on animals anymore— at least I like to think they're rarely used on animals any- more—the ability to find a trap that has that used, antiquated look (the kind of look that just screams *tetanus!*) is a bit dif- ficult.

Traps can be obtained from a variety of places, including magic shops, some of which cater to sideshow folk as well (an entertainer is, after all, an entertainer). However, note that there's no gaff about an animal trap. There's nothing about a spring animal trap that's deceptive at all. You want an an- imal trap that can break bones, and that's what you're getting. There's no secret switch that'll make it safe. There's no lever that'll slow down the closing mechanism of the mouth to make it less painful. This is a trap—a true animal trap—that's really, really shiny.

The newness of the trap is the first thing that strikes me when our instructor produces one. Not that that should ac- count for anything. The trap is just as dangerous if it's new and shiny or old and rusty. But, still, it'd be nice if it had that old, used look to it. Maybe a bit of dried blood around the mouth would add to the theatricality of it. Looking at the trap I'm already thinking to myself, "It's small and on the light side. With the right routine one could, feasibly, do wonders with it and amaze an audience."

The trap is set by placing it on the ground and pressing down on the outer part of the trap with the foot. The mouth is then pushed open and the catch slid into place. You can then carefully pick the trap up. As long as you don't touch the catch, which is the center pad where any bait might be placed, you're safe and the trap won't snap shut.

Our instructor places the trap on a stool and produces a pencil, which he jams into the trap. It springs shut quickly and loudly. Even more impressive than the actual snapping shut of the trap is the affect it has on the harmless I-wasn't-hurting-nobody pencil. Not only does it break it, but it shatters it into hundreds of tiny wood slivers and chips. No, "shatters" is the wrong word. Obliterated is better. The pencil is obliterated. There are bits of wood everywhere.

Later, after I've obtained my own trap, I try something a bit harder and use a plastic pen. The results are the same. The mouth of the trap causes the plastic casing of the pen not just to break in half but to splinter the plastic at the point of impact.

I imagine for a moment that this is my finger. Not only would it break my finger, but it would most likely break into numerous smaller pieces in the area of bone that takes the brunt of the impact. An unpleasant image on numerous levels, I imagine attempting to shuffle a deck of cards or sign my name on a check with a cast on my hand. An even more disconcerting image is the one where I mistakenly put two fingers into the trap the wrong way and have them both broken.

Other than the burns I'd given my lips when fire-eating, for the most part I'd gotten through the week unscathed. However, if this was done incorrectly, the resulting injury would be nothing like the burns my lips had received from the torches that would heal in a few days. Most likely, it would be weeks or possibly onward of two months before any broken bones were fully healed.

The trap is reset and our instructor explains how every trap has a sweet spot, a spot in it that if you hit it just right, you can have the trap snap shut on your hand with absolutely no danger to you at all—which, I know, is complete and utter crap.

He poises himself at the trap, holds his hand above it, counts off quickly, and jams his hand into the trap. There's a moment as a spectator watching this, just a moment after the trap has sprung, when you're convinced that every bone in the hand has been broken. It lasts for just a moment until the person begins the task of working the trap open again to release his hand. There's no screaming. No crying. No begging to call 911. Rather, it's just an unpleasant situation in which you're trying to extricate yourself—or so it seems.

Having done this several times since, I'm not going to say it doesn't hurt at all, but there is a way to do it without breaking any actual bones, and, again, the answer lies in the science and principles used in both lying on the bed of nails and walking on glass.

If you were to insert a single finger or even two fingers into a trap, they would most likely end up broken. However, if you were to jam your entire hand into the trap, you've now increased the space over which the force of the trap is coming down. You're spreading out that force over more area, not just a single, vulnerable finger. With more area to absorb the blow, there's less chance of getting seriously hurt. The key, however, is to place your hand into it just the right way. Timing and the way you put your hand in is everything. Get it at the wrong angle, and you'll be faced with a fist full of broken fingers.

Now, again, the potential for great routines oozes out of the trap, but there's more that can be done with other types of traps as well—a mousetrap, for example. As I found out at *Sideshow Gathering*, the use of mousetraps is another thing that can be done. What, you may ask, can be done with a mousetrap? Jamming your entire hand into a mousetrap might seem like it would be painful but not all that challenging. Alright then, how about your tongue? Yes, you've set it on fire; now let's jam the poor thing into a mousetrap. It's a strange set of circumstances that led me to seek out the ability to snap a mousetrap on the tongue. It all began with Facebook.

When I started using Facebook, I had no idea whatsoever what I was doing. I knew that I wanted to set something up where I could network with other performers, specifically some of the folks I'd been meeting who were performing the sideshow skills I'd learned thus far. I'd heard tell of Facebook, but, for some time, labored under the impression that it was something teenagers used as a form of communication, the Internet equivalent to texting if you will. While some of this is basically true, it also only scratches the surface of what Facebook truly is.

In any case, I joined Facebook. Once a member, you need to acquire a group of friends with whom to communicate. Otherwise, it's kind of like going to a party, finding the one empty room in the house, and hanging out there all night while everyone else is downstairs.

So I dropped a few "friend requests" to people I knew, none of whom were performers, and then followed it up with a few requests sent to magicians I was familiar with. Then I received a request from Jason Black, of *999 Eyes*, whom I met during the latter part of the summer on Coney Island. That got the ball rolling.

You see, once you've started acquiring friends, Facebook then suggests people you might either know or want to be friends with because they're friends of friends you already have. That's how I came to know Casey Severn, better known as Dash to his Renaissance Fair audiences.

Severn started out as a professional actor and stage combatant at *Renaissance Faires*. He was introduced to *Renaissance Festivals* while in high school, and upon graduation, he embarked on a tour of the United States with a *Free-Flight Birds of Prey Exhibition* show. Once he began working faires regularly, a certain amount of boredom set it, and to combat this boredom, he taught himself to eat fire. While not the recommended method, he caught the eye of another performer who was also there, Johnny Fox, who showed him there was more he could do with fire than just sticking it in his mouth, and that fortunate encounter began to open up more performance options. That's when the sideshow and the skills usually associated with them began to draw him in.

"I think that mainstream America may think on the sideshow

as its 'Dirty Uncle Tommy,'" Severn said. "The 'Dirty Uncle Tommy' who makes rude jokes and farts during dinner engagements. Nobody really talks about him the rest of the year, but when he comes to town for a visit, you feel yourself fill with excitement, while your parents are always happier when he leaves."

Severn began adding to his repertoire of sideshow skills and learned the Human Blockhead act, the Bed of Nails, the art of walking on broken glass, a bullwhip act, and some feats using animal traps. He began playing with traps, from mousetraps to wolf traps, tinkering with a variety of presentations. With these stunts, Severn knew that the most important part was the ability to increase the anxiety audience members felt by making what he was doing look more difficult and painful than it actually was.

"During my Animal Trap act, after I put my hand in the wolf trap, I ask for audience members to try to open the trap off my arm. Usually, they can't open the jaws. At the *Gathering* this year I chose poorly. I picked the guy with all the muscles. Regardless of whether or not he should have been able to open the jaws, the jaws were opened. I learned at that point: pick the little skinny guys to try to open the trap."

Prior to attending the *Sideshow Gathering*, I stumbled onto a picture of Severn on his Facebook page with a mousetrap on his tongue. By this point, I'd already eaten and breathed fire, was regularly hammering nails and other objects into my nose, and was working on the basics of sword-swallowing. Given these facts, after seeing someone with a mousetrap on his tongue, what would you do? I know, what does all this say about me?

While at *Sideshow Gathering*, I didn't have a chance to connect with Severn, but while there I was able to catch Gwyd the Unusual snapping a trap on his tongue during his act. I was even more intrigued and turned to both these men to walk me through snapping a trap on your tongue.

Gwyd, it turns out, not only snaps traps on his tongue but snaps numerous traps on his tongue, one after the other—not one, not two, not five, not ten. Gwyd holds a record for snapping nineteen traps on his tongue within a minute's time. Now that's *got* to hurt. It makes you wonder what the tongue is like after a stunt like that. The answer is, not good.

"It was about one to two inches thick and bruised literally black," Gwyd recalls. "I couldn't talk properly for about twenty-four hours, that's when it finally went down to purple. It throbbed like a toothache for the first twelve hours. I got off the stage and everyone was offering me drinks, but all I wanted was ice cream. To this day I still have dents in the sides of my tongue from doing it. But as soon as someone beats that record, I'll do it again."

So, does it hurt? Yes, it does. *Believe me.* Don't get me wrong, snapping a trap on your tongue hurts in a whole different way than a burn from the rod of a flaming torch, the most painful thing I experienced at Sideshow School. It goes without saying that I was being as safe as possible. But still, the worst and most painful injury I received was the torch burns on my lips.

Snapping a trap on your tongue is an entirely different experience. It hurts quite a bit, and that's an understatement. The pain is exquisite, quick, and sharp. And much like the bizarre meal consumed by Violet Beauregarde via a stick of chewing gum in *Willy Wonka and the Chocolate Factory*, you end up tasting three things at once.

The first thing to hit you is the taste of the wood on which the trap is built. Mousetraps are built on small rectangles of fairly cheap but sturdy wood that's similar to plywood. These aren't finished in any way. So when your tongue contacts the wood, it has a rough, unfinished feel to it. And the taste is, well, it's woody, kind of like you just jammed a box of toothpicks into your mouth.

The second taste that you get is metallic. This comes from

your tongue contacting two points on the trap: the first being the catch that causes the trap to snap shut and the second from the actual bar that makes up the trap and slams shut on your tongue.

The third taste is the sweet, tangy, coppery taste of blood. Because what you're doing is snapping a trap on your tongue. The snap of the trap bursts capillaries and blood vessels in your tongue, so you're liable to taste some blood.

The first day I attempted this feat, I sat at my kitchen table with the trap set. I'd pick it up, place my tongue in the trap, and gently work at the catch or trigger. I was actually able to flick my tongue gently against the catch without setting the whole thing off, which, in many ways, made the anticipation associated with the actual snapping of the trap all the worse.

So I'd flick my tongue against the catch; then, for fear of the trap actually snapping on my tongue, I'd pull it away. The initial shock of the trap snapping and the anxiety of the moments before it happens are more terrible than the trap actually snapping. I did this several times, placing my tongue in the trap and fiddling with the trigger with the tip of my tongue without actually causing the trap to snap. Then, finally, I did it by accident.

I'd wanted to be able to get in front of my computer and have it take a picture of the trap on my tongue, but the initial reaction my body had—and the fact that my tongue was covered in saliva—caused the trap to slide off my tongue more quickly than it had gotten on there. I jammed my tongue in, the trap snapped, and before I knew it, my hands were pulling it away. A black line across my tongue was the only evidence that it had happened at all—the black line and those three wonderful tastes in my mouth, that is.

Now there are inherent dangers in snapping a trap on the tongue. The placement of the tongue is exceedingly important. Should you place your tongue in the trap in a way that's wrong, several things could happen:

The first is you could lose the tip of your tongue. I'm thankful that this is a moment I've yet to experience. I'm not looking forward to the day a trap snaps shut and I watch the tip of my tongue fly from my mouth and across the room as if I'd received the Heimlich maneuver from someone at a steakhouse. But like I said, that moment thankfully hasn't happened yet. And if all goes well, it never will.

The second potential hazard lies in the lips. Either your top or your bottom lip could easily get caught in the trap when it snaps if you're not careful. Not as bad as losing a chunk of tongue, but still not something you want to be shooting for when you're doing this kind of thing.

Finally, and almost up there with losing a piece of your tongue, is the fact that the mousetrap is made of metal and is so powerful that it makes it all too possible for you to end up chipping a tooth if this act isn't performed correctly.

"My mouth has taken the brunt of the damage throughout the years," noted Donny Vomit, of the *Coney Island Circus Sideshow.* "I have broken teeth on mousetraps... and managed to snip the tip of my tongue off in a raccoon trap once. It has grown back, but I still have no sensation of taste there."

Things you don't want happening when you snap a trap on the tongue, and very good reasons why, if you were looking to learn a feat such as this, it's important to find someone who can teach you how to do it and do it correctly.

CHAPTER NINE

~∾

THE FREAKOPHILES PRESENT BRIDGING THE GAP BETWEEN THEN AND NOW:

Ward Hall, the *999 Eyes Freakshow*, and Penn Jillette—Step Right Up, Step Right Up!

Most people go through life dreading they'll have
a traumatic experience. Freaks were born with
their trauma. They've already passed their test
in life. They're aristocrats.

—Diane Arbus

Gibsonton, Florida, is some thirty to forty miles just south of Tampa. It's a little town that few people have ever heard of, and if you were to ask your ordinary run-of-the-mill elementary school, high school or college student, they probably would never have heard of the place.

This is a fact that I find inherently bothersome, and the level at which this annoys me increases the more I ask people about the town. Consistently, whenever I bring up Gibsonton in any conversation, whether it be with the performers I meet or laypeople I am giving details of the book to, I get the same response: "It's not what it was."

What was it? That's a good question. Given that Gibsonton is probably significantly different than it was twenty, thirty, or even forty years ago, it's difficult to get a definite sense of what life might have been like in Gibsonton. Yet with the few facts we have about the town, something of a picture can be gleaned.

Situated south of Tampa, but just fifty miles north of Sarasota, which was the headquarters of the Ringling family (of circus fame), Gibsonton, Florida, was the wintering home for many circus and sideshow folks such as Al and Jeanie Tomaini. Al was a giant for the circus, and Jeanie had been born without legs. Eventually they retired to Gibsonton, where they opened a restaurant, The Giant's Camp, and became active in the community, with Al becoming fire chief. It's also believed that Gibsonton had the first post office counter scaled down to accommodate the customers who lived in the area who were little people. Gibsonton provided a home for people who spent most of their year traveling with circuses and sideshows.

Long after Sideshow School had ended, I made my way down to Gibsonton for a brief taste of the place and the opportunity to interview one of its residents. As I'm told numerous times from the moment I arrive in Gibsonton to the time I leave, most of the freaks and more unique circus folk have passed away, leaving little of what Gibsonton used to be intact. Yet, show folks still live in the town. Driving down Gibsonton's streets, you pass one home that has a Tilt-A-Whirl in its yard, folded up and sleeping until the next carnival season comes around. And rather than your typical businesses, there are places here and there offering to rent out any variety of rides and other carnival and fair equipment you might need.

It is in this place that I find Ward Hall, one of the last true sideshow men. I pull into his drive and take in his modest ranch-style home. In the front is a small swimming pool, and on either side of the house are trailers for carnival use. In front of one of those trailers lies a large, circular wooden frame used for knife throwing.

Behind Hall's home, and just over the fence, is the neighbor's yard, in which is growing a beautifully rich orange tree. The leaves on the tree are full, lush, and green, and against these leaves hang plump, bright oranges, which, when juxtaposed against the green of the leaves, make them all the more striking. Beneath the tree sits a fried dough stand.

I make my way to Hall's door to learn more about the man who has made most, if not all, of his living in either the circus or the sideshow. He answers the door and at seventy-eight years of age speaks with a vitality and love of life you rarely see in someone his age, and as memories are recalled, one story leads to the next, which invariably leads to the next. The first story he relates to me makes me question my beliefs in fate and destiny and makes me wonder whether our lives on this earth are set in stone from the moment we are born.

"When I was three or four years old," Hall said. "Now, my mother told me this. We lived in Nebraska, and it's very cold. This was early in the Depression and we were dirt poor, and my grandmother had lost her house, and was living with an aunt, so we moved in and rented two rooms from my great grandmother. The kitchen was kind of in one of these big rooms. And it was a cold January day, and my mother was working in the kitchen, and I took two of the kitchen chairs and put them back-to-back and threw a blanket over them. And I'm underneath there, and my mother said, 'What are you doing under there, Ward?' And I said, 'I'm playing in my circus tent.'

"They never could imagine where I had heard the word circus or how I knew about a circus tent because I had never seen a circus. They had never talked about such a thing, don't know if they'd ever seen one. There was no television, of course, it was 1934. We didn't own a radio until I was seven, and there was no movie theater in that town. We didn't get magazines or newspapers—my father would go to the barber shop to read the newspaper—so nobody could ever imagine where I had heard the word circus or construed a circus tent. So somehow, I believe, that I was preordained to be in this business because from my earliest time I wanted to be a circus performer, but I never saw a circus until I was eight.

"My parents separated when I was seven, and my mother took us—I had one sister—to her parents in Illinois. A year later, I was by myself and I went by myself to the circus. It was Barnett Bros. Circus, and I know all about it now, because I studied it. I went to see that circus and I was eight years old. I had just had a birthday, and that was the first circus I saw."

Hall's first circus memory eventually led him to the memory of the first sideshow he witnessed—a year after seeing his first circus.

"The next year, when I was nine, I saw another circus, and that was Lewis Bros. Circus. Now, I don't remember anything about a sideshow with Barnett Bros., but Lewis Bros. had an independent sideshow, it was a carnival sideshow (a sideshow that's usually booked with carnivals), but it was booked on the circus and was owned by a guy named Ted Metz. I remember standing watching the bally, and some stranger, when the people were going in, said 'Would you like to see that?' And I said, 'Yeah, but I don't have a dime.' And he said, 'Here's the dime.' So I got to see the sideshow.

"But like many carnival shows in those days, it was what was called a Pit show, they didn't have stages, they performed in a pit, so you stood and there'd be a rail there, and I'm pretty sure that I must have got up close to the rail. But the thing I remember, because it was right in front of me, was the tattooed man. And the only other thing I remember about that show was that they had a man who balanced furniture on his chin and walked up and down a ladder."

Growing up in the midst of Depression-era America, Hall easily recalls the way in which many stores and shops in both cities and towns would be open for business one moment and closed the next, leaving behind empty and vacant real estate that ultimately became utilized by circus and sideshow workers.

"Store shows were very popular during the Depression and before that to the time of P. T. Barnum. Barnum had a permanent sideshow in New York City which was called Barnum's American Museum. It was started in 1843. There were also permanent museums, which had sideshow acts, in Boston, Philadelphia, Baltimore, all the big cities. Then in the 1930s, they were very popular. First of all the fair season would close, or the circus would close, and nobody had any money to speak of, and at that time the people didn't own any homes anywhere, and they had no place to go, and when the season closed, they wondered what they'd do then.

"So somebody came up with the idea of the store show, and it worked very well. There were a lot of empty store buildings in the Depression years, and you go rent a store building for a month or for a week or whatever, on the main street in town, and then you put up advertising, some of them were quite organized and had circus general agents in the wintertime booking them, circus bill posters, and they'd bill it like a circus, and the store shows were pretty strong performances.

"When I was nine years old, it was Cash Miller who had a store show that came to Illinois. In that show he had an Indian, and he had a guy that imitated Popeye, and he had a sword-swallower, and a magician, and a pinhead. That's all I remember about it. But I remember that magician, I was very impressed with him, and I know now, that that was Walter DeLenz, who was from Coney Island. Walter DeLenz was the king of the magic pitchmen until Marshall Brodien started pitching Svengali Decks on television. Marshall was the highest paid magician of all time, and all he did was the Svengali Deck. But Walter would show the tricks, put them in a bag, and he sold the bag of tricks for maybe a quarter."

All of these experiences ultimately built a foundation on

which Hall would build a career in both the circus and the sideshow.

"I was thirteen, my father had come through Illinois and took me back to Nebraska, and at that time I was also living with an aunt who was very good to me and for me. She taught me how to write a business letter and taught me how to type. So it was spring break at school, and that week Johnny Howard had his store show, and at that time I had a few dimes in my pocket, and it was a dime to get in, and I would go every day, and hang around there, and they had a guy by the name of Don Taylor who did a ventriloquist act and also sold the magic packages. Well, I had a quarter to buy one of his packages, so I did.

"Well eventually a little circus came through town. I spent the day around there, saw the show. And I saw an ad in a newspaper, they needed clowns. And as I said, my aunt had taught me how to write a nice business letter. So I wrote them a nice letter, and of course didn't tell them I was only thirteen, and I got a contract back and I showed it to my dad and said, 'Look I'm going to go to the circus,' and he said, 'No, you're not. You're going to stay here and go to school.'"

And it looked like that was the end of that. But looks can be deceiving. His father's business ultimately took Hall to Colorado, and it was while he was there that he heard that the Daly Bros. Circus was going through Boulder.

"Daly Bros. Circus was routed into Boulder. I caught a bus in the early morning and went up to Boulder. And when I walked on the lot someone said, 'Hey kid, you want to work and get a free circus ticket,' and I said, 'Hell, yes.'

"So I went over and talked to Bill O'Day, and it was the sideshow. I helped put up the sideshow, and saw the circus. But I wanted to eat in the cookhouse, and so I said, 'Do you need any help to travel with the show?' and they said, 'Yeah.' So they hired me at thirteen.

"But this was a lie, I had no intention of going with the

circus, but I wanted to meet all the people around there and eat in the cookhouse. Now, from what I saw, unlike Cole Bros. on which I'd worked a year before for a very short time as a prop hand, Cole Bros. was highly professional and had big-time circus acts, and I could see that they were the place you went after you learned something. But Daly Bros. was the kind of a show where you'd go and they'd teach you something. And I was right."

Returning home, and to school, Hall bided his time until the season came around again, keeping his eye on the newspapers for ads until one finally caught his eye.

"The next spring I saw the ad that they wanted a Fire-eater and Punch and Judy for the sideshow. So I wrote them a nice letter and told them I wanted $30 a week, a berth on the train, and cookhouse. And I got a telegram back: SALARY OK. SHOW OPENS APRIL 1ST. JOIN ANYTIME. WINTER QUARTERS GONZALEZ, TEXAS. SIGNED MILT ROBBINS. So I quick went down and made some fire torches, and through trial and pain I learned to eat fire a little bit."

At the age of fourteen, accepted into the circus, Hall was wise beyond his years, and immediately began planning other ways he could make money while working for Daly Bros.

"I remembered those two magicians I'd seen in the store show selling those packages of magic, and thought 'I could do that.' And, of course, the one I'd bought I really knew how to do those little tricks and knew how they were made. Well, in Denver, in those years, there were a lot of hotels in downtown Denver before the days of motels. And everything was downtown. So one day a week I would put on my suit, and I would make my rounds of the hotels. Every hotel in the lobby had a writing desk and I would go and sit down at the writing desk, and make out like I was writing something. I'd look around and keep watching, and when the time was appropriate, I would steal all the stationery and go to another hotel.

"After I had acquired enough stationery for my supply I would go back home to my room and with my scissors I would cut off the letterhead and I would use the stationery to fold up the Chinese coin vanishers, and make the vanishing flower and whatever else. I'd cut out the doll and paste it on the back for the shadow dance, and so by the time I got ready to leave to go to the circus, my uncle in Denver had given me an old steamer trunk. Now, I didn't have many clothes, and I had one piece of wardrobe I found in the goodwill store, but I had plenty of room in there to put magic packages, so I had a trunk full of magic packages.

"So on opening day we're getting ready to open, and I said, 'Mr. Robbins, would it be alright when I do the magic act if I was to sell some novelties?' And he said, 'Novelties? We've got a novelty joint on the midway. What kind of novelties?' And I said, 'Well, I've got some magic tricks I'd like to sell.' And he said, 'Oh, you want to pitch?' And I had never heard the word before. I said, 'Yes.' And he said, 'The package doesn't cost more than a nickel to make does it?' I said, 'No.' 'What are you going to sell for, a quarter?' I didn't know. I said 'yes.' He said, 'Fine, then I get a third.' I said, 'Fine.' And I was in business the first day I was in business."

It was in 1948, at the age of seventeen, that the Rogers Bros. Circus hired Hall, and it was there that he'd get to manage his first sideshow.

"The manager of the sideshow was Carl Stone. Nice guy, and his wife was a sword-swallower, and they had two little kids. Nice family, except that Carl was an alcoholic, and about every three days, he would miss the next day because he would get drunk. So, after the first time he got drunk and nobody seemed to know what to do.... I took it upon myself to go out and make the bally out in front, and make the opening."

Hearing what happened, the manager of the circus told Hall, "The next time Carl gets drunk, I'm going to run him and I want you to take over the sideshow." Hall simply agreed, and was told that he'd be getting an additional twenty-five dollars a week. Little did he know that he should have been getting a percentage.

"About three days later Carl got drunk again, and I said, 'Give the guy another chance. He's got a lovely wife and two little kids, and he's promised he's not going to do it again.' But, of course, three or four days later he did it again, and so I became the sideshow manager."

During his career as a showman, Hall worked for sideshows connected with both circuses and carnivals. In the carnivals, there'd be a variety of different shows attached to it in addition to the attractions owned by the carnival itself. These shows, such as sideshows and single-o's (attractions featuring only one exhibit), would rent space on the carnival midway. Hall recalled one of these shows from a carnival much later in his career.

"Mark Williams was over there and he had a beautiful little show. It had a forty-foot front on it with a little trailer, and it was *Vampira: Dracula's Daughter from Ecuador.* And the words 'Dracula's Daughter' had blood dripping off the letters. And he went for ten cents in those days. And he was the first person to have an endless tape for the tape recorder. They hadn't invented it yet, so Mark had had his sleeping quarters at one end of the trailer, and on the wall by his bed he took spools like sewing thread spools and had fastened them onto the wall. Then he would take a strip of tape that he recorded, it was a reel to reel, and he could get thirteen words or however long that would be, and he'd splice it together, put it into the head of the recorder, and then wind it through those spools up on the wall, and so it was constant, and long before they invented it.

"Hal owned that carnival and was a wonderful guy, and had a great sense of humor. And Mark was up checking in his money to the office one night and Hal happened to be in there, and he said, 'Looks like you did pretty good today, Mark.'

It was a Saturday in Atlanta, and that was one of our big days. And Mark said, 'Yeah, I had a good day.' And Hal said, 'I don't know how you can afford the nut of that show'—the nut being the expense of putting on the show. Hal said, 'It must cost you so much money to operate that show, I don't see how you can make a profit. My god it must cost you fifty cents a day to feed that vulture.' Because that's what it was in there. People came in and saw this big vulture."

Oddly enough, the peak of the life of the sideshow carnival parallels the life of Gibsonton, Florida, itself.

"Probably the 1930s, 1940s was the peak of Gibsonton as far as sideshows were concerned, and 1948 was the first carnival sideshow that I had. At that time, according to my inaccurate research, there were 104 10-in-1 sideshows working in North America at that time. At the same time that I'm talking about 104 sideshows in the business, there were in the carnival business over 4,000 shows. And out of the 104 sideshows, there's only one left with carnivals, and that's ours."

Hall, along with his partner C. M. Christ, operates *Hall & Christ's World of Wonders*, which travels from one carnival to the next, making its way from Florida all the way up to Minnesota during the course of a season.

"People often ask, 'What happened?' Was it that the public wouldn't support the shows? Or political correctness setting in about the girl shows and the freaks? That never had anything to do with it. The business declined on the carnival simply because in the early 1950s some carnival owners, mainly Patty Conklin in Canada, found a place called Europe. And they discovered that in Europe, they'd had these big elaborate rides since before the turn of the twentieth century. And there were manufacturers over there that built these big rides.

"Patty Conklin was one of the first guys to bring a couple over here. And then Charlie Copper had the first Himalaya-type ride, not nearly as elaborate as the ones you see now, but I remember he was on his way to play the Canadian National Exhibition in Toronto, and he had a week open, so he jumped into Cold Water, Michigan, with the *World of Pleasure* shows where I was at that time. When they set that up, and we opened on a Monday night, everybody on that carnival, the sideshow people, all the concession people, we left our businesses and went down and stood in front of that Himalaya to see when they turned on the lights, which mainly was a bunch of light stringers then, and started the music. Little did I know at the time I was looking at the first nail in the coffin of the carnival shows. Because it was like a vacuum, it just sweeped up the money, and sucked it in."

Sideshows as well as other shows that rented space on carnival midways would pay 54 percent of their gross to the carnival. Four percent was for insurance, and the other 50 percent was for rent. But carnivals quickly saw the purchasing of rides as a shrewd business tactic. Rides were an investment because rather than renting out space and receiving 50 percent of someone's gross for that space, they could replace a sideshow with a ride that they themselves owned. Therefore, 100 percent of what that ride brought in went to the carnival owners. In addition, even the biggest rides didn't take five men to operate, so it meant less people to employ, cutting costs in another area as well. Rides changed the face of carnivals and changed the face of the world of sideshow. Over time, circuses, sideshows, and carnivals evolved and changed, just as Gibsonton itself evolved and changed. As time went by, many of the performers who'd worked in the traveling shows passed away, instilling in Gibsonton a truly unique history.

On the day I am leaving town, I stop to get gas for the rental car, and I get into a conversation with the man pumping the gas. It's early morning, and he seems as if he's been there all night. But he's wide-awake enough to engage in some small talk, during which he tells me that the town isn't what it once was. He even goes so far as to say, "It ain't nothing now."

This is when the bothersome and annoying feeling first crept up on me. Truly there's more to Gibsonton's past than just some fading memories. I wonder if Philadelphia were any less famous being that Benjamin Franklin and other members of our Founding Fathers are now dead, or if the importance of Washington, DC, were diminished being that many of the presidents who passed through its streets and its monuments were now gone. How does one gauge the importance of a man? Is a president any more important than a giant?

Somewhere between the memories that seemed locked within Gibsonton's past and its future there is a life beyond what it is today. A life that can only be known as its future unfolds. One can only hope that the future recognizes and embraces the past because somewhere in Gibsonton, the past is alive. It's part of history, the history of the circus, and certainly the history of the sideshow. Gibsonton and showmen like Ward Hall are tangible links to a past and history that sideshow performers today are following.

As I leave the gas station, as I put Gibsonton behind me, I glance in the rearview mirror and watch the gas station attendant stretch and crack his back as another car pulls in behind me. Public perception isn't always right, and just because public perception seems inclined to see Gibsonton as less than it once was, it doesn't make the place any less historic.

It was public perception, after all, that labored under the belief that the real reason for the death of the sideshow—or at least the decline of the sideshow, since we know its not dead—had to do with the outcry over the exploitation of women in the girl shows and the people involved in shows that displayed genetic anomalies. This was far from the case. But people believe that to this day, a fact that the *999 Eyes Freakshow* is seeking to change.

I first became aware of the *999 Eyes Freakshow* on Coney Island while watching Jason Black ply his trade on the sideshow stage there. He took the stage wearing black pants, a black T-shirt, black cowboy hat, brightly colored sneakers (as any performer will tell you, comfortable footwear is a must), and a black mask reminiscent of the Lone Ranger. Scrawled across the T-shirt in white letters were the words 999 EYES FREAKSHOW. It peaked my curiosity, so I made contact with them and found my way to Samantha X, the person who is one of the co-founders of what is one of the few true freak shows in existence today.

"The *999 Eyes Freakshow*," Samantha explained, "started when I agreed to build a freak show tent to highlight the history of freaks and to sort of reclaim the word freak again to mean a genetic human anomaly and help the new sort of resurgence of circus underground culture to remember some of the freaks of the past rather than just remembering the tattooed people of the present but the actual genetic human anomalies of the past. And while I was putting this tent together to go on tour with an underground circus, I met the Lobster Girl, and she began working with me on the tent. We then attended a *Yard Dogs Traveling Road Show* and met Deirdre the Dancing Dwarf. So after we met Deirdre the dancing dwarf, we decided to put out an ad."

The ad they decided to place was more about building a bit of buzz about the project they were working on, with the hope of attracting attention to their freak show tent. The ad began like this: DO YOU HAVE SKIN CONDITIONS, EXTRA LIMBS, FACIAL DEFORMITIES, MISSING LIMBS... Their Elephant Man, Ken Pittman, stumbled onto their ad and applied for a job. His birth condition, neurofibromatosis, is one that is genetically inherited and causes tumors to grow over much of the body, so for him becoming part of *999 Eyes* was a life-changing event. Never having been a performer prior to joining the group, Pittman learned what it took to be onstage, and once he became comfortable, encountered a change in himself.

"With the speech impediment I get ridiculed a lot," Pittman

said, "because a lot of people think I might be stupid. And being on stage gives me a chance to say, 'Hey, I'm a very intelligent person even though I have a speech impediment and I've got bumps on my body. This is me.' Before I was hiding, hiding all that. And I was afraid to touch a lot of people, or even take off my shirt, and I had a hard time being myself.

"The show has really helped me out a lot. After a show, I have people come up to me and say, 'I saw you outside, and I didn't know what you had, I thought you might be contagious and I didn't want to come near you.' And after the show, they're coming up to me with tears in their eyes, giving me big hugs, and all that, telling me, 'Your story touched my life so much.' That's what makes it worth it."

With Pittman suddenly on board, they were a traveling museum of three freaks, at which point they began traveling on the side of a larger show that included knife-throwing performers, fire dancing, as well as other variety acts. It was early in 2005, and *999 Eyes* had just begun.

"Halfway through that tour, we did a radio interview where I said the same thing, it was called the freak callout: 'Do you have skin conditions, extra limbs, facial deformities, missing limbs, are you a little more interesting than that 10-toed, 10-fingered blueprint of human existence? Then come on down to the show tonight, and you can jump right onstage, then jump right on the tour bus...,' and Jackie the Human Tripod Girl showed up that night ready to go. She said, 'Okay, here I am. I've got a karate act, I'm going on tour.' And we said, 'Well, don't you want to talk to your mom?' since she wasn't even twenty-one. So she literally just hopped on tour with us. Fortunately, we're a super, super tight group of people and very community based."

By the end of the tour, Samantha began receiving letters from people asking if they performed separately from the larger show to which they'd been attached, something that just focused on the freaks. And that was the moment when the freak show was truly born as a separate entity.

"Because the three original freaks had never performed and a lot of them were hiding their anomalies and had been raised with a stigma around their birth condition, it was the birth of an amazing show and being able to watch each of them turn into amazing performers."

As the show evolved as a whole, it began to take on a life of its own, displaying many of the traits typical of a vaudeville show.

"We believe we're the only vaudeville freak show in all of history."

In the show, as is vaudeville tradition, everyone has their own act and everyone in the show interacts; for example, the Lobster Boy, Jason Black, does a stand-up comedian routine and is a magician as well, but on top of that, he also interacts with the other performers in other skits during the show.

Once the vaudeville structure of the show was determined, they pushed each of the performers and all the skits and routines to fit that structure. This included creating a band to back the show. The band, dubbed That Damned Band, was born out of the show. Their accordion player and one of their founders, Dylan Blackthorn, writes most of the music for the show, and the musicians not only provide music for the show but also interact with the performers during the skits.

As each routine developed, they attempted to integrate the performers as much as possible in the vaudeville tradition, yet at the same time giving each freak their own time in the spotlight, highlighting their individualism.

The Elephant Man does real-life stories from real-life freaks, in which they recreate the past in order to remind audiences that at one time it was socially okay to go and listen to someone tell his story about being different rather than being ignored or put into institutions or living off the welfare system.

The Human Tripod is a fabulous jazz singer, is an acrobat, and does karate demonstrations. Little Miss Firefly, the midget of mischief and mayhem, has done many, many acts in her life from aerialist to suspension to dancing to glass walking to fire-eating. She's multitalented. Lobster Girl does a classic vaudeville skit, with corny punch lines, and T-Rex the flipper boy, does whip tricks and is the drummer in the band.

Laurent the Clown, who is also one of Samantha's main partner in organizing the show, also acts as the show's clown. But his talent doesn't end there. In addition, Laurent also does many acts including a fire act, high-velocity hot dog cannon, and other routines that help string the show together since they usually have several plots running through the show at the same time. Amazingly—and thankfully—*999 Eyes* has had only a positive reception.

"We had one disability rights group concerned about our choice of the word 'freak,'" Samantha recalled. "Our response to them was we'd like to see them work to eradicate the word 'disabled.'"

Samantha describes the show as one in which the audiences have the tables turned on them. Believing they'd be attending a show in which the performers would be the ones empowered (they are), the show ultimately empowers the audiences as well. Through each skit, each routine, and each act, *999 Eyes* outlines the ways in which they find ten-toed and ten-fingered people boring. Samantha puts it best by saying, "Freaks are nature's art." This framework, driving the audience toward this belief, ultimately shatters the audience's preconceptions of not only what is beautiful, but what is *normal.*

The *999 Eyes*, in the great tradition of the freak show and sideshow, celebrates the uniqueness of the individual. Not only are they highlighting the importance of their own uniqueness, their own birth conditions, and the genetic anomalies that made them different, but they're reminding audiences at the same time that there was a time, not so long ago, when people often celebrated being different, conjuring an atmosphere where people like Al and Jeanie Tomaini are far from forgotten. In America, the individual is exceedingly important, and they remind us of that fact. I find it hardly a coincidence when I speak with Penn Jillette, of Penn & Teller, that this is a fact he believes in as well.

A number of years ago, just prior to Penn & Teller setting up shop at the Rio in Las Vegas, I had the opportunity to see them twice, once in New York City and once in Philadelphia. Both viewings came on the heels of having discovered the *Coney Island Circus Sideshow*, and I was struck by how strongly Penn & Teller's show was influenced by the sideshow, to the point that, at the time, they were performing an illusion that included Penn crammed inside a barrel with rods jammed through it. Audience members were then offered the opportunity to see how Penn fit into the device, all for the cost of a bright, shiny dime. Ring any bells?

Early on in their careers and up until 1992, Penn & Teller ended their shows—including their run on Broadway—with the 10-in-1 monologue, in which Penn extolled their love of the sideshow. The monologue wrapped up with Penn eating fire, but the entire routine was laid out very carefully and condensed the feelings he had regarding the sideshow, as well as highlighting the incredible influence the sideshow has had on the team that is Penn & Teller.

When Penn speaks, three things are abundantly evident: the first is his love of performing, the second is his love of music and his vast knowledge of musicians, and the third is his love of the sideshow. Though, it should be noted, none of these things come across necessarily in that order.

"The thing about the sideshow that I always feel is the most important thing to say, the way the sideshow affected me and changed me and the way it inspired me, is a very big distortion of the real sideshow. When I listen to the Velvet Underground, I listen to them without any ideas about heroin. When

I listen to Jimmy Hendrix, I don't think about LSD at all. And those are driving forces in those two things. But because I never had a sip of alcohol in my life or even a puff of marijuana, it's not part of my world. So there's a Velvet Underground and a Jimmy Hendrix that live inside my head that don't really overlap with the real ones at all.

"When I used to go to the sideshow in Greenfield, Massachusetts... publicly or professionally and artistically when truth is not called for, I talk about being drawn into that world and really loving it. The truth is, I'm just a little less artistic or just a little less quick. I was afraid to go in. So I just stood outside the sideshow and listened to the talkers and listened to the grind tapes over and over again. So what I really love is not so much the sideshow but the talking *about* the sideshow."

His fascination with the talkers is something that quite obviously made an impression on Penn, as it's something that seems to have reverberated throughout his life, with ripples touching on the stage show as well as the critically acclaimed and award-winning *Penn & Teller's Bullshit* the duo produces for Showtime.

"I always prefer the story to what really happened, which may be why I have an obsession with truth. I lean naturally in the way of enjoying fabrication so much, but I enjoy fabrication that's closer to truth. I don't enjoy fantasy at all."

Penn's first foray into performing came in the form of juggling.

"When I learned to juggle, I'm fifty-three years old now, so I learned to juggle when I was about twelve, so that puts you in about 1967, and that's before Hovey Burgess and juggling became a hippy, college student, Colorado Hackey Sack thing. At that time juggling, at least to a kid in a dead factory town in Massachusetts, was exotic and almost a sideshow skill. I had never met anyone who knew how to juggle. Never. Ever. I didn't know anything. I just set out with brute force to be a juggler. I was already a passably good juggler—I mean by those standards, certainly not by today's standards; by today's standards it's ridiculous—before I ever saw a juggler perform live."

With more than a passing interest in the sideshow and juggling, the young Penn soon turned his attention to fire-eating.

"I would read about fire-eaters, and I would hear talk about the Human Salamander, and I would see the sideshow posters and on and on and on, before I ever bothered going in and seeing a fire-eater. And I was taught absolutely nothing, and to give you an idea of how old that monologue was when I was doing it on Broadway and there was all the whoha about it, I taught myself fire-eating with no skills whatsoever and not even so much as an *incorrect book*. I was eighteen and took a coat hanger and wrapped a rag around it and stuck it in gasoline and just started sticking it in my mouth and burned my lips until they were entirely white and blistered with no real lip left, and got to learn some basics about it.

"And in a just perfect, almost cinematic story, I was doing my monologue about the sideshow and fire-eating, and I was talking about what it meant to me to choose to be an outsider. Because it's one thing to be a freak and have that kind of thrust upon you, but choosing it's a slightly different thing. And that's a lot of what the monologue's about. So I wrote the monologue and ended it with fire-eating. And I was doing that in 1974 or 1975 in Philadelphia, when a guy showed up to our show in some outlandish outfit like a top hat and cape. After the show—the show was in a room that's a hundred seats and was maybe half full, that'd be optimistic—came up to me afterward and said, 'You know that monologue you do about fire-eating is really, really great. Shouldn't you be a better fire-eater?' That was Doc Swan. And Doc said, 'You're a really good juggler and a really shitty fire-eater. Why don't we get together and you help me with the juggling and I'll help you with the fire-eating.' And I went out and I learned fire-eating from Doc Swan after I had been doing it profession-ally for a year and a half."

Eventually Penn made his way through the various sideshow working acts, some the very ones taught at Sideshow School. But it was sword-swallowing that he attempted to not only learn but also perform on television—in one sitting.

"For our first Public TV special that was called *Penn & Teller Go Public*, it was in 1984 in Los Angeles, I brought in a guy called the Baron who was a real sideshow guy....I brought him into the studio and thought maybe I could learn sword-swallowing with just brute force on camera with him teach-ing me. It turns out that brute force on sword-swallowing is not your best choice. What I did was, on camera over the period of forty-five minutes, pretty much forced a sword all the way down my throat. There was a lot of vomiting, and there was a lot of pain, and I bruised the sphincter down at the top of my stomach, in the middle of my chest, and you don't do that when you learn fire-eating. With sword-swallowing, you learn slowly over a period of several days or even weeks, and learn the relaxation. You learn to think about it; you don't essentially force the sword down your throat. So I did real damage to myself. I've not gone back to sword-swallowing since mostly because I just don't have a bit for it that isn't exactly the same as the fire-eating bit or doesn't cover ground that other people have already covered."

Penn soon discovered that he was not alone in his love of the sideshow. He and his new partner, Teller, worked together for *Renaissance Faires* and sated their mutual interests in their off time.

"Our very first time working together was 1975 or 1974. We did the *Minnesota Renaissance Festival*. It was our very first time; Teller had just quit as a high school Latin teacher, and I, of course, had nothing to quit because I couldn't do anything but wash dishes. We traveled out to Minnesota to do the

Renaissance Festival and the Minnesota State Fair was playing there at the same time. And that was when Teller and I started our obsession.

"What we would do was—we were working Saturdays and Sundays, and then Mondays, Tuesdays, Wednesdays, and Thursdays of the week it was in town we went to the Minnesota State Fair every day. We would pay our seventy-five cents… and we would go in and watch the show, I don't want to exaggerate, but certainly three or four times and go in three or four times a day and do that. So we'd watch it twelve to fifteen times a day."

The sideshow may have appealed to each of the performers, but being individuals what they saw, how they saw it, and what they took in—how they processed it if you will—was completely their own. And just as he had in his youth, Penn, now an adult, was just as strongly attracted to not only the way in which the outside talkers plied their trade but the way in which the performers inside the tent did the same show over and over again.

"I was just really interested in what happens to talk when you repeat it enough that the sounds are memorized but the meaning no longer goes through your head, and there's a kind of depth in reality. What I was fascinated by in the sideshow was the fact that you had your sword-swallower, your blockhead, or as you'll see the act doesn't matter, and you've got somebody that was probably in that tent because he had a beef with the law, or he was an ex-con or he was a fag at a time when he shouldn't have been a fag. They were all on the run in some way, and go into this job, not because of a burning need to be famous, like John Lennon or Elvis, and not because of artistic expression, like Bob Dylan, but as a job. And then they would use lines that had been repeated by people over and over again, and the originator was forgotten. And they'd kind of not understand some of them, and not get the wording right on others, and kind of strip it down in this oral tradition, and then just kind of repeat it. And after they had done all that, there's some sort of human meaning that came across to me.

"That's what the sideshow was to me. More than the kind of standard stuff you hear about, and that I talk about, about being different and living outside, and Robin Marks, that interests me so much less than what happens in the oral tradition of poetry. I love the guys who wrote their acts when they were fourteen and were still doing the act word for word when they were sixty.

"I'm fascinated by a guy with the audience changing, grinding out show after show after show. And it's one of the reasons I'm obsessive about always making sure there are big hunks of our show that we've been doing for thirty years with very few changes. Now there's also stuff in our show that we wrote two weeks ago. But I think that one of the things I really miss from culture is that there are fewer people repeating stuff because of essentially the ability to cut and paste. Now with our text, we can cut and paste and you don't have to type it again. And Norman Mailer would have argued and indeed did argue to me that writing it out in longhand then typing it up and having to write it again in longhand actually brought something to the writing that word processing never could."

The grind, the repetition of the show, and the language and the acts over and over and over again meant something to Penn and continues to mean something to him to this very day. It's a kind of repetition rarely seen in this day and age.

"The excitement of doing something the first time and seeing something the first time, the excitement of improvisation is certainly there but seems much cheaper to me. I just like the human depth that you get with the repetition and the grind.... Juggler Michael Goudeau once said, 'The variety arts are for people who watch *Ground Hog Day* and think that looks like a great life.'"

While his love of the sideshow stems, on one level, from the way in which these shows and acts were grinded out in a repetition that was based in an oral tradition, there is another detail of the sideshow that also appeals to him and, in many ways, is at odds with these facts. And that is the way in which America has infused itself into the sideshow and made it its own with the way in which it values the individual.

"It seems that I'm directly contradicting myself by loving the grind and the fact that it's handed down, and then going directly to individualism. But the American idea, the idea that the rest of the world just doesn't get, is how important the individual is to America. We love our individuals. And what I love about the freak show, because the part of me that most likes the American philosophy is the part that loves the individual.

"What I love is the fact that if you're going into the sideshow and you're seeing a little person or you're seeing a hermaphrodite or you're seeing a seal boy, flipper boy, or lobster boy, or any of those things, you're seeing someone that's just so clearly saying—and this is exactly the same as Thomas Jefferson—I am a complete and utter individual and that's what we're coming here to celebrate."

The sideshow has evolved and changed quite a bit since P. T. Barnum got his hands on it and created something new and American with the idea. But, in many ways, it hasn't changed a bit. From Ward Hall who spent his youth and, ultimately, most of his life in the circus, carnival, and sideshow world, to *999 Eyes* and even Penn & Teller, the sideshow has influenced and changed the American landscape and, by the same token, has been influenced and changed by the American landscape.

For a long period, from the 1950s until today, there were veritably few actual freak shows in existence. And *999 Eyes* has brought back that tradition, a tradition started before Hall got into the business, but certainly a tradition that he was a living, breathing part of and certainly a tradition that Penn not only got a taste of but believes in quite strongly.

Sideshow performers are not only part of a long tradition but part of a tradition that is very much orally based, handed down from performer to performer, even though many sideshows don't exist as they once did. But the tradition is still there, and it's still alive. But these performers aren't only part of that tradition but also part of an American tradition. An American tradition that, in a most uniquely American way, celebrates individuals and all they have to offer.

Jason Black of *999 Eyes*, better known as the Black Scorpion and the Lobster Boy, celebrates that tradition every time he steps onstage, pulls off his gloves, and allows every member of the audience to bear witness to his birth condition. Because it is who he is and no one can strip him of that.

CHAPTER TEN

⁓⌣⁓

SIDESHOW SCHOOL, DAY FIVE: SWORD-SWALLOWING,

or, Down the Hatch Without Even a *Little* Scratch?

Mean people suck, nice people swallow.
> —Natasha Veruschka,
> The Queen of Swords

In my show I only swallow one sword, and the reason is that any more than one sword is just boring the audience. It's asking the audience to sit there while you stroke your ego. And there's no need for it.
> —Roderick Russell, sword-swallower

Less chitchat, more swallowing.
> —Natasha Veruschka,
> The Queens of Swords

The inherent problem with sword swallowing is my friend Eddie Gardner of Diamond's Magic Shop. On my return from *Sideshow Gathering*, I bring my computer over to Eddie's place to show him the photos I've taken. Being the *Sideshow Gath-*

ering, the pictures produce pleasant, though visceral responses from him. Seeing someone display a bit of a frisson on seeing a bizarre or unusual stunt such as jamming needles into your arm or sticking your face into a shower of sparks is partly the reason I was attracted to sideshow stunts in the first place. To give someone that thrill—a thrill that's both pleasing and, at the same time, repulsive or chilling—is a gift. And the folks populating the photographs from *Sideshow Gathering* have that gift in spades.

Then I come to a picture of someone swallowing a sword, and Eddie deflates like a balloon. The edge-of-your-seat tautness to his body disappears. The borderline worry and anxiety that defined his face moments before evaporates. He's nodding to himself, as if he were in the know. He's nodding to himself as people in the audience of a magic show might nod when they've convinced themselves they've figured out how the most recent miracle was accomplished. Then Eddie utters the one word that must be the bane of all sword swallowers: "collapsible."

Magicians are liars—honest liars, true, but liars nonetheless. If you watch them perform a trick and you figure out how it's done and confront them on this fact, their best defense is to lie through their teeth. The secret must not be divulged, and no one must see you sweat.

With the skills I learned at Sideshow School, I'd assumed I was free of all that. These were skills that could be learned and mastered. There was no deception. And if someone, anyone, confronted me about the secret behind such a stunt or routine, there was no need to lie. There was no need to cloak my answer in deception. There was no deception. Yes, I hammered a nail into my nose, and it went deep into my head. Yes, I removed my shoes and socks and walked on glass. Yes, I ate fire, and yes, I filled my mouth with a flammable fluid and breathed it into the air above my head.

There is no deception, yet there are people who still believe that there could be no other explanation for such stunts than deception. Hammering a nail into your head? The nail must fold up. Walking on glass, there must be an invisible sole you wear to protect your feet. And the best of all: you eat fire? There's a special chemical fire-eaters use to make it look like fire. It's called cold fire. It's harmless. All these explanations are both laughable and demeaning to the performers who have, quite literally, taken months if not years of their lives to master such skills. People have a right to be skeptical. In a world where people claim to speak to the dead and bend spoons with their mind, it's understandable that there must be some level of skepticism. Therefore, it's the performer's job to convince the audience as best he can that what they're seeing is as real as it gets.

Stephon Walker, as Swami Yomahmi, before walking on glass takes a fresh bottle and shatters it, spreading the shards among the pile of already broken glass, and Todd Robbins even allows audience members to examine the bottoms of his feet before going for his stroll.

For the most part, anyone who has seen an actual fire-eater and believes he is dealing with something as ridiculous as cold fire has had the wind taken from their sails because the heat from the torches and any fire breathing can be felt from the stage to the seats. Harley Newman's fire-eating and breathing routine not only allows you to feel the heat rolling off the stage, but it allows you to smell the stench of the fluids filling the theater so that you might think you're at a barbecue gone awry.

Therefore, it is with great trepidation that I delve into the subject of sword-swallowing because it is the one sideshow skill that I find most audience members—most laypeople—believe to be a trick or deception. I am disappointed when I come to realize that my friend Eddie is not unique in his response, many people fully believe that sword-swallowing is the sideshow equivalent of a card trick or sawing a woman in half. There must be deception involved, which is a belief that requires the sword-swallower to work that much harder and frustrates me, a potential swallower myself, to no end.

And what increases the frustration level even more is actually to come across a gaffed sword that allows an audience to believe you've swallowed a sword, something that Robbins really uses in his own act to show the difference between a real sword and a gaffed sword. That's when I realized that sideshow performers are almost like lawyers, having to prove things to their audience long before the audience can accept what they're seeing and what the performer is doing—though I'd pay good money to see a lawyer swallow a sword. In fact, I'd put down good money and bet that many people would pay to see a lawyer swallow a sword. The fact that the lawyer ends up not succeeding might be totally beside the point.

On our last day of Sideshow School, we're promised the very basics of sword-swallowing. I must admit that while many of the skills taught gave me something of a fright prior to learning them, sword-swallowing was the one thing that intimidated me the most, and not because, once you learned it, you were dealing with unbelieving audience members. Rather, the actual act of inserting something that large into your body, into your mouth and down your throat, bothered me on a very basic level. It seemed both invasive and penetrating the way a possible surgery might make me feel.

True, I'd already learned to hammer a nail into my nose, which, once learned, seemed easy. But this was *different*. This was deeply invasive on a primal level. When you hammer a nail into your head, you can move about, talk, smile, nod, any variety of things—safely. Insert a sword into your body and there's very little you can do. In fact, if you insert a sword into your body and make a wrong move, the result could very well be internal bleeding.

Shockingly, the last day of Sideshow School consists of many things, mostly recaps of what we'd already learned, the answering of any questions we might have, a bit of history on the sideshow, and, of course, the sword-swallowing—which, even more shockingly, takes up a minimal amount of time.

Since Sideshow School, I have seen my share of sword-swallowers, some of whom actually work the item with which we trained into their act: a wire hanger. We take the hanger and bend it in just the right way and clean it well enough so that it can be used in lieu of a sword.

The trick here is to overcome the gag reflex, which takes some time. How much time? Longer than a day? Longer than three days? Longer than a week? To be fair, once I was halfway through the work on this book, I began a ritual where every day before sitting down to write, I attempted to get the hanger into my throat. Two months later, I was only at the point where I had completely overcome my gag reflex. This didn't mean I could swallow the hanger, the sword, or anything else. All this meant was, I'd overcome the gag reflex and could safely seat the hanger in my mouth, where it rested nicely against an obstacle. I was unsure what this obstacle was until I spoke with sword-swallower Roderick Russell.

Now thirty, Russell started sword-swallowing in his late teens.

"It developed not so much as an interest in performing, as it did an interest in pushing my own limits as a human and exploring my own boundaries. I've always had an intense interest in the nature of consciousness, in addition to the intellectual study of what consciousness may or may not be, and how to control it, how to experience it. I have enjoyed running experiments on myself to push my own boundaries and push my own buttons."

Unlike the folks at Sideshow School who, at the very least, were given some direction with regard to where to begin when it came to getting something down their throats, Russell started on his own.

"I'd never seen a sword-swallower in my life, never seen a sword-swallower in a book, never seen one on television, nothing. But as we all do, I had the general conception of 'sword-swallower' in my mind. We all sort of know what it is. Without ever having seen anyone, I decided to see if I could put my mind to the task of achieving it."

He first tried to make connections with sword-swallowers who were already established performers. But what he found at the time was that most people who practiced the art of sword-swallowing weren't very forthcoming with information about it.

"In the early years I spoke with Dai Andrews a little bit, I went to a couple of his shows, I made a trek, and we had dinner, but we really didn't work together in terms of learning sword-swallowing. But I definitely, by watching what he was doing, picked up on some subtle tips and tricks of the actual process.... Most of my research was done through book reading."

Yet, as Russell soon found out, there was very little written with regard to instruction on the subject. What there was he consumed, then turned his focus to his own body, concentrating his research on his own physiology and anatomy.

"I've learned very well the different parts of the body I would be affecting, different things that could go wrong, things that could go right. I really put a lot of work into the science background, the science aspect of it. Because I wanted to make certain that if I were going to do this, granted it's a dangerous act, but if I were going to do it, I was going to do it as safely as I possibly could."

When he thought he was ready, he went online and blindly ordered a variety of swords. Not using anything with which to train, such as a hanger, Russell slowly attempted to swallow a dagger.

"I started the process of poking and prodding, and I always had to relax myself. I used to practice yoga regularly, and I'd stretch quite extensively, and I'd breathe and calm myself, and then I'd try to swallow the sword. And I did all sorts of bizarre things. I'd just lower the sword into my body and start coughing and gagging. I'd try different positions. I'd bend over slightly. I'd hyperextend my neck. I'd move my body into all sorts of bizarre positions just to see if anything would allow it to go down easier. And what I'd do is I'd lower it as far as I could into my mouth, and I'd place my finger on the blade right where the blade met my upper lip, and I'd keep lowering it until I got to a spot where I couldn't push past, whether it be because of an obstacle or because of gagging. And when I'd reach that point, I'd lock my finger into place, pull it out of my mouth, and see how far it was. I'd measure to see how far it was and I kept a log."

For nearly five weeks, Russell kept up this ritual, getting in no more than five inches of the blade. "That's nothing," he says. "That's like a toothbrush."

"And then finally, one day, I got it down to five and a quarter inches, and I celebrated. But it was a very, very slow process. And it got to the point where I could reliably get to seven or so inches, six and a half or seven or so down into my throat. And I was no longer gagging, but now I was running up against an obstacle. And I had no idea what this was."

This obstacle, it turned out, was exactly the same obstacle that I'd come up against—the epiglottis.

"I knew that I'd be able to push past it eventually. There's nothing in my way. It closes when we hold our breath, it closes when we eat. I knew it can close, so I knew I could push past it, but I just psychologically wasn't able to get over the sensation that I was being blocked and couldn't get any further."

For Russell this period corresponded with a trip he'd been planning to make to Italy.

"I got in touch with someone in Italy, Thomas Blackthorn, and when I flew over there—he'd been sword-swallowing for many, many years—I arranged to meet with him. He gave me some pointers, and I also brought my blades with me. And I was working with one blade in particular. It was a twelve-inch-dagger, and I just couldn't get this thing all the way down. So I asked him, 'Would you mind swallowing this for me, just so I can see that it's possible to swallow this sword in particular?' I felt that if I saw someone swallow it, I would know in my mind and in my gut that yes it's possible, there's no reason that I can't do it as well. So he swallowed it for me with no problem whatsoever.

"He actually had me swallow one of his swords, and it was a *hugely* long sword. To this day, I can get it all the way down to my stomach, but I still can't swallow the whole blade because it's just physically too long for my body. He's much taller than I am. So he has more room. This is when he gave me the pointer of actually swallowing."

What Blackthorne suggested to Russell was, once he came in contact with the epiglottis was to swallow—actually to go through the physical act of swallowing.

"I popped that blade up, his blade. I licked it and put it up and lowered it down as far as I could go, and I ran into the same obstacle that I'd been running into, my epiglottis, and I couldn't push it any farther. And that's when he told me, when the blade was actually in my throat, he said, 'Just swallow it.' And he literally meant actually swallow. I did that. I made the motion of swallowing. I gulped it down, and sure enough, my throat grabbed onto that sword and yanked it straight down into my stomach, and boy, that was uncomfortable. And that's an understatement.

"Then when I flew back to the states, I finally was able to get the twelve-inch blade down as well, all the way to the hilt. And then I was able to do it repeatedly. After I was able to do it the first couple of times, the process of getting comfortable with it came fairly quickly. The blockage I was running up against was much more passable once I got past it the first time. With every time I got it down after that, it became easier and easier and easier."

Through his research and through his continuous swallowing, Russell became well versed in the path the sword takes when he swallows as it goes through the body starting with the pharynx, which is at the rear of the mouth.

"This is where you need to tip your head to precisely just the right angle, and what I found in the early stages was that the blade has to be on the back of my tongue. And pushing hard down on the back of my tongue, I throw my head back and I slide it down. And when it touches, when it gets past the back of my tongue, actually into my throat proper, into my esophagus, the pressure is such, and the angle has to be such, that there is an enormous amount of pressure on my front teeth. My head wants to be pushed forward a little bit, the front teeth are contacting the blade, and the back of the tongue is depressed quite severely, so there's a huge tension point there. And that tension point has to exist in order to have the proper alignment to push it down.

"Now as you become more accustomed to it and things start to loosen up and you start to feel a little less nervous about it, there's not as much tension. You have wiggle room, more play, but especially in the beginning stages, there's that huge fulcrum point that I had to work with. And it was very uncomfortable.

"Then it gets down to the epiglottis, which was the major obstacle I was running into. The epiglottis is a huge obstacle because when it's open it's effectively blocking the passage of anything down into the stomach. That's part of its role. Part of its role is to block things going down into the stomach that aren't supposed to. Part of its role is closing over the trachea so that when you eat, nothing goes into there. So when it's open its point is up at an angle. So what has to happen is the epiglottis has to be pushed closed, but I found that the easiest way to do this is to hold the breath momentarily because that'll make it close naturally. And once it closes, you can push straight past it and then resume breathing again. Now you can't breathe quite as well because the epiglottis can't open all the way, so the air going into your lungs has to go through a smaller passage. That said, you can still breathe, and you keep the sword in indefinitely as long as your body doesn't want to reject it."

Once beyond the epiglottis, the sword, it turns out, comes very close to the spine within the esophagus. "You are millimeters from the spine in your neck, because your head is thrown back, putting a curve in your spine, and the esophagus passes just in front of the spine. And if you were to ram it down at all, you would forcefully contact the spine and probably do some serious damage.

"The esophagus is a very thin membrane. People are sent to the emergency room all the time because they choked on a tortilla chip that punctured their esophagus, or various other nonthreatening foods. They cause major problems because the esophagus is so very thin. So it doesn't matter how dull or how sharp the blade is, it's just as dangerous."

From this point on, Russell pointed out that there aren't nearly as many obstacles as the first few you encounter when first swallowing (gag reflex, coughing, epiglottis), yet there are certain things that can be unique to one's own anatomy that could cause problems.

"The obstacles from here on out aren't so much obstacles as they are dealing with uncomfortable sensations. I seem personally to have an issue with it."

It turns out one of the problems Russell had when sword-swallowing is the blade of the sword, quite literally, brushing up against his heart as he pushed the sword lower into his chest.

"The esophagus is straight, but it's not exactly sword straight, and so what happens is the blade inside the esophagus will push the esophagus slightly forward, and it'll make it impact the back of the heart.

"I did some X-rays at the Central New York Medical Center, and I didn't know that that's what it was until we're all standing there, me and a group of doctors, we're all looking at the X-rays we'd just taken. Everyone's marveling at them, and a cardiologist who wasn't involved with the event at all, he was walking through the hall and he stopped and he looked, and he said, 'Wow, you can see the back of the heart is pushed *flat* by the sword.' And he pointed it out, and sure enough, on the lateral X-ray you can see my heart is flattened on one side."

When something such as this happens inside the body, it can't happen without repercussions.

"Imagine when you're coming off a very intense routine," Russell says, "and your heart is pumping quite hard, and then you have to swallow the sword. That would make it even worse. What happens when I get to the level of the heart with a sword is I get this sensation throughout my entire body that feels very much like a hot flash, like when a hot flash goes over your body and makes you momentarily go a little woozy, it's exactly like that, except there's no hot involved. It's more like an electrical wave. In all other respects, it feels pretty much the same as a hot flash, and the best that me and the doctors can figure out is that it's due to the sudden change in blood pressure, because the heart is pushing against the sword through the esophagus and it's collapsing and compressing the chambers of the heart so it's dramatically changing the blood pressure, which is momentarily making me go lightheaded and woozy."

After passing the heart, the sword then comes up against the cardiac sphincter.

"The cardiac sphincter is that valve on top of the stomach. It's what prevents acid from coming back up from the stomach into the esophagus. It's slightly cocked to the left, because the stomach is more on the left side than it is on the right side. So the fact that it's slightly cocked to the left means that the blade's not going to go straight into it, you have to sort of shift a little bit, or wiggle the blade around a little bit to get it lined up just right. I nudge it, I push it open, and it goes into the stomach. My blades are just long enough to sit just above the bottom of the stomach."

After speaking with Russell and hearing of his experiences with regard to the X-rays he'd had taken with a sword intact, I was even more curious about the further dangers that might be faced when swallowing a sword. I turned, once more, to Evan Goldman, Ph.D., of Philadelphia University to find out what the inherent dangers were to sword swallowing.

"One could cut the tonsils or arches at the back of the mouth or the lining of the esophagus," Goldman began. "I would expect that the sudden pain would cause an extremely unwanted reflexive 'jerk' which would result in further damage. A major knick in the wall would require surgical repair....It is not a straight path through the mouth, down the esophagus, and to the stomach. There is the obvious sharp turn at the back of the mouth; then there is a small curve near the opening of the trachea. There are upper and lower esophageal sphincters that are typically closed (and could easily be damaged by a sharp object). The aorta causes the esophagus to angle slightly toward the midline, and immediately before entering the stomach, there is a curve back to the left. Plus, the esophagus, especially behind the trachea, is flat anteriorly/posteriorly. I would expect... [a] sword would follow all these curvatures without a problem (straightening the esophagus as it goes), but a sharp tip or edge would be very damaging."

In addition to your run-of-the-mill risks that are faced when thrusting a sharp steel object down your throat (internal hemorrhaging, punctured esophagus, damaged cardiac sphincter, etc.), when you begin the process of building an acceptable and entertaining presentation further complications can arise. Tyler Fyre of the *Lucky Daredevil Thrillshow* recalled an incident in which he was attempting to swallow a sword crafted completely of neon. "This particular neon sword was brand new to me, and it was the first show of the day at noon on

a Sunday on Coney Island with only eight people in the audience, and I wasn't giving it my all. I wasn't lined up just
right, and the sword broke when it entered my stomach. The
light went out on the handle, I heard an earth-shattering
CRACK, and thought to myself, 'Well, this is the moment I've
always wondered about.' I pulled the sword out, and thanks
to a genius idea by my neon guy who put a piece of fishing
line inside the glass tube, I was able to retrieve all the glass.
Unfortunately, that involved pulling broken glass up my esophagus, which cut me up both sides from my stomach to the
back of my mouth.

"Interestingly enough, the audience didn't care that they'd
just seen a rare moment in sword-swallowing and a near-death
injury onstage. After two weeks of drinking aloe vera juice
and whiskey (not at the same time), I was back on solid food
and swallowing swords soon after that. Now I no longer swallow a neon sword, but I give my all at every single show so
that if anything goes wrong, it'll be a spectacular accident at
a great show."

Todd Robbins also reiterates the danger of swallowing neon
swords, having had one break inside of him as well. A bit more
lucky than Tyler, Robbins was able to retrieve the sword from
his throat without a scratch, but to this day still does not
swallow neon.

One performer who does, however, is Natasha Veruschka.
By all accounts Veruschka is both a unique and talented performer, weaving the art of swallowing and belly dancing together.

"When I started out, I was a very well-known belly dancer.
I'd always perform with a sword. Swords on the hips, swords
on the head. And it would always balance."

It was actually through belly dancing that Veruschka made
the leap to sword-swallowing, feeling that in many ways this
ancient art actually chose her.

"I was the feature belly dancing performer. There were

about eight other belly dancers, and I'm the feature performer and my teacher at the time never asked me to be in her troupe. I was always a soloist. And my teacher was getting more and more jealous because I'm getting more and more jobs. She had her favorites, and her favorites looked like her. And I was so out of the realm, but it didn't bother me. It bothered her. So I finished my performance and I had my sword and I kissed the sword at the end because I did such a great job. It had been balanced on my head, they're heavy, and I'd done such a great job. And this teacher went crackers on me. She was so upset, that she said 'Don't you ever kiss that sword again,' but she said it onstage and I left the stage crying. Crying. And I was very quiet. And that night it was like an epiphany. I knew in the morning, I'm not going to kiss the sword again. I'm going to swallow it."

This set Veruschka off on the path to learn how to sword swallow. Seeking a mentor, she found John Bradshaw from Virginia, who aided her in learning the art. Trained by Bradshaw mostly by phone, he walked her through how to begin sword-swallowing.

"I tried one rusty one," she recalls, "which is really stupid because it can pull your insides out. It actually *will not* come out. It had all these beautiful intricate carvings, and when you put it down, it adheres to your insides. So I started to take it out, and tugged, and tugged, and tugged and my insides were coming out. I could feel it. And I thought 'I'm not going to get this sword out,' and I'm losing breath. And I thought I'd have to pull it out totally—BOOM—or bit by bit by bit. So I did BOOM like a Band-Aid. It was terrible. But now I'm doing twenty-nine inches."

Veruschka began sword swallowing in 1995. By the year 2000, she was sword-swallowing and belly dancing full time, finding the experience of performing a rewarding one.

"I've performed all over the world. And when I performed in Lebanon, I was on Lebanese television three times a day over and over and over for months. But when I was performing in Lebanon, there were men with rifles who would come because it's a different part of the world, and when I performed I saw Jewish and Arab, young boys, young girls, there were Catholics, there were old people, young people, and everybody came together, there was absolutely no turmoil. And I didn't say, 'You can't come in and watch me with guns.' You know, they had guns strapped to them, some had swords, and everybody got along. There were no worries. There wasn't any problem with these people together, which is really amazing, and I notice that a lot. Their differences go away.

"I was in China and about four people fainted. They were all men. And no one bothered to pick them up. They just kept watching me. And I don't stop the show for anything or anyone. I just don't. I've had music crap out on me; I still keep going. I've had my costume fall off me, totally fall off because I'd be belly dancing too hard and my costume's too big and I'm too small. It dropped right off and I kept on performing. I've had my shoe break; I keep on going. I've stubbed my toe once really bad, fell off a chair while I'm doing it in the audience and kept on going. So these four men fainting, it was a large audience, I kept on going. When it was over, the audience looked down and poked them and told them it was over."

Eventually, Veruschka became so skilled as a sword swallower, that not only was she featured in *Ripley's Believe It or Not* but also in the *Guinness Book of World Records*. She holds a total of seven world records: (1) The most swords swallowed at once (13 22-inch-long swords, a Guinness Record); (2) the most swords swallowed at once by a group (50; Natasha downed 11 swords, Guinness Record); (3) the longest sword swallowed by a female (27½ inches long, Sword Swallowers Association International [SSAI] World Record); (4) the only female "Neon Sword Swallower" (24 inches long, SSAI World Record); (5) the only female "Sai Weapon" Sword Swallower (24 inches long, SSAI World Record).

Recently, Veruschka broke a new world record. National Sword Swallowers Day was celebrated on February 28, 2009, and at the *Ripley's Believe It or Not* location in Times Square a number of sword-swallowers gathered. It was there that Veruschka swallowed a 29½-inch steel sword.

And when it came time to tackle the neon, Veruschka turned to sideshow man and artist Johnny Meah for advice about how to get the bulb down. Hesitant to give anyone advice about such a dangerous act, "He told me if there's anyone that's going to learn this properly, it's you." After signing off on a waiver for Meah exonerating him of any liability should something go wrong while she swallowed the neon, she received careful directions from him as to how to go about it.

"The first place I got the neon I didn't get it from Johnny, I had to have it made. The first place I got the neon made does the biggest neon signs in Midtown Manhattan, and they light up Broadway. Now, they're no fools. I come with a sword design, they're not idiots. Once again, there's a waiver if anything happens.

"We come home and I take the sword out and put it on the sofa, and I go, 'Oh, my God it's beautiful.' I pick it up and it cracks. That's how delicate it is. A thousand and fifty-five million pieces. I put it down and I'm in shock. I call up the glassmaker, 'I need another one.'"

After having another one commissioned, Veruschka picked up her second neon sword.

"I take it home. Gingerly, I plug it in and I look at it. I unplug it. I plug it in and I look at it. I put it to my lips, and I put it down. You can*not* be frightened."

Many risks go along with neon that can cause such fear. Unlike other swords, a neon sword has a whole batch of problems that go along with the fact that you're swallowing a glass sword that lights up and gets plugged in.

"The heat from it [is intense], if you're onstage a long time. I've had emcees who won't get off the stage; meanwhile, the sword is lit getting hotter and hotter and hotter. By this time it was so hot, but I then did my whole routine, and it burned my insides and adhered to the inside of me.

"The other problem with it is differences in temperature. If your body is too hot and it's too cold, it explodes. Also, if you're too tense, your throat closes up over it, and it can crack. So now I have this beautiful sword on the couch, and it's lit up, and I look at it. The next day I try to swallow it; I can't do it. So I put it back on the couch and lean it on the couch right by the shoulder of the couch, and it broke. Twenty-five-million pieces. Again. Call up, 'I need another sword.' They made a fortune off of me.

"I got the neon. And there was no way I could swallow it. My manager says to me, 'I don't want you doing this.'"

But Veruschka was determined. Sword-swallowing had become part of her. "I feel whole when I swallow swords," she notes. Therefore, she continued the battle to swallow neon.

"It just wouldn't go down, I just couldn't do it. I had the neon sword for two years and I couldn't swallow it. And my manager goes, 'You can just put it on the wall.'"

Whether a comment such as that bothered her or not, it was on New Year's Eve in 1999 that she finally steeled herself to accomplish what she had not already done. However, it took a tremendous amount of emotion to get from point A to point B.

"On New Year's Eve 1999 I asked my manager, 'Before you leave, because it's the last day of 1999, I need you to plug the neon in.' I look at the sword. And I do a really stupid thing, I call up my family, my adopted family."

Having been adopted and brought up by a Mennonite family, she'd since been shunned for having left the community. "So I called them up, stupidest thing, and they had shunned me, which means I was dead to them. So I called them up, and they always called me 'Barbie' because I looked like a little Barbie doll. And they denied knowing me, and said there was a grave they made for me. And I was buried, so who was this impersonating me?

"I'm going, 'No, it's me, don't you remember your little Barbie?' And they go, 'No, we buried little Barbie.'"

At this point the emotion peaks for Veruschka, as she's crying into the phone. "I'm screaming, 'GOD, THIS CANNOT BE HAPPENING.' It was like I didn't exist."

And, after the call, feeling saddened and distraught on the last day of 1999, she attempted to swallow the neon sword, bringing it to her lips and slowly lowering it into her body, succeeding at something that up to that point, she'd been unable to accomplish.

She's seen other tragedies in her life as well due to sword-swallowing. "I almost died. I lost 53 percent of my blood. I'm lucky I'm alive. My swords scissored on me, and it was horrible." The scissoring of swords is another risk swallowers face. When inserting more than one sword into the throat, there is always the risk of the two swords sliding apart in different directions, thus forming the shapes of a pair of open scissors while inside the body. The resulting scissor formation causes the blades to rip through the esophagus.

Heather Holiday of the *Coney Island Circus Sideshow* mentions this fact prior to swallowing two swords at the same time, using the swords to demonstrate the way they might scissor while inside her and stating the fact that she might actually die. Few audience members might not entirely believe this fact, but the danger and risk involved is all too real. Before dropping the blades into her body, she recites the sword-swallower mantra: "Down the hatch without a scratch." One can only hope.

The moment two swords pass anyone's lips—a single sword for that matter—they immediately place themselves at risk, which makes the feat all the more dazzling, all the more daring, and all the more *important*.

The performers I met with all agree on one thing: presentation is everything. In addition, a sort of equation seems to emerge when you examine the stunts, feats, and skills these performers are displaying. The equation goes something like this: the presentation of the stunt should be equal to or greater than the inherent danger of the stunt being performed, thus increasing the gravity and importance of the entire routine.

While I consider myself lucky to have seen numerous talented sword-swallowers, there are others I've come across who treat the effect as a passing fancy or a quick trick, all of which not only diminishes the ancient art they are performing but also diminishes them as performers.

Whether it be as entertaining a presentation as one can give such as can be found in the way in which Damien Blade and Heather Holiday perform their sword-swallowing routines, or the way in which Roderick Russell crafts his more theatrical stagings, or the way in which Tyler Fyre and Thrill Kill Jill's routine is infused with thrill-show adrenaline, or the way in which Veruschka has woven the two ancient crafts of sword-swallowing and belly dancing together, the important key to not only sword-swallowing but any routine lies in the way in which you give of yourself when it comes time to structure your presentation.

"Do nothing without love and appreciation," Veruschka notes, "and from a place of *feeling*, either sad or happy."

As I come to a close on the sword-swallowing chapter, I think of the way in which the very basics of the craft were taught to us in Sideshow School. These basics are the pinpoint tip of a massive iceberg lying dormant and cold beneath the surface of a turbulent ocean—*a pinpoint tip*. With sword-swallowing there is much to learn. Those who practice this art make it look easy, simple, entertaining, and dangerous all at the same time.

With my research strewn across the table, I stop typing and

go to the living room, where I poke and prod my throat. The gagging and coughing has subsided. Tears no longer spring to my eyes when I insert something that deep into my mouth while my head is tipped back. Yet I'm still running into the obstacle, still coming up against the epiglottis that blocks my way. It is an obstacle that I'll overcome, as I overcame the Blockhead and as I overcame my fear of inserting a flaming torch into my mouth.

But overcoming the obstacle and sliding something down my throat is only a few inches farther beneath the surface of the water. Once I learn the physical act, there is so much more to do to give the act its own weight and *importance*. I tip my head back and try again. "Down the hatch, without a scratch." A better mantra might be, "Do nothing without love and appreciation, and from a place of *feeling*, either sad or happy." I'm intend to do just that.

~~~

CHAPTER ELEVEN

THE FREAKOPHILES PRESENT MISFITS IN THE LAND OF MISFITS:

A Brief Snapshot of the Modern-Day Sideshow—Alive! On Stage! Now!

The good old days are now. *You have to make your own damn history.*
    —James Taylor, author of *Shocked &*
    Amazed: On and Off the Midway

Sideshow Gathering takes places once a year in Willkes-Barre, Pennsylvania, in conjunction with a tattoo convention aptly named Inkin' the Valley. *Sideshow Gathering* is one of the few places you can find sideshow performers from all over the United States converging on one stage for what seems to be marathon sessions of lightbulb eating, lying on beds of nails, hammering nails into nostrils, chowing down on night crawlers and live gold fish, sword-swallowing, whip-cracking, and other sundry sideshow fun. One moment Crispy of the Crispy Family Carnival is waiting for audience members to staple $1 or $5 bills to his torso ($20 if you want to staple the bill to his forehead), and the next, Doc Wilson is walking blindfolded through a sea of animal traps. It's just another day at the *Sideshow Gathering*.

Oddly enough, *Sideshow Gathering 2008* took place on the weekend before the 2008 presidential election, one of the more historic in our country's history. To make the weekend even more David Lynchian (or Salvador Dalian depending on your artistic tastes), I found myself reading Sarah Vowell's fascinating book *Assassination Vacation*, in which she details her visits to the sites related to famous presidential assassinations.

I was led to Vowell's book by the musical that partly inspired it, Stephen Sondheim's *Assassins*, which also addresses the theme of presidential assassination. Only Sondheim does it in song. Honestly, what more can you ask for than a duet between John Hinckley, Jr., and Lynette "Squeaky" Fromme à la Neil Diamond and Barbra Streisand's "You Don't Bring Me Flowers"? I'll tell you what, a show that ends with the characters opening fire on the audience. All this and more in *Assassins*! You've *got* to love musical theater.

Now, if you had a moment to either listen to the radio or watch television during that period, you heard about little else other than the race between John McCain and Barack Obama. In the weeks following the election, it was a relief not to have campaign ads cluttering up the rock radio station. David Bowie's "Rebel Rebel" loses a bit of its bite when it's bookended with ads that end with the words "and I approve this message."

But during *Sideshow Gathering*, with the election just a few days away, in my off-hours I paged through Vowell's book and mused over these men and women who have etched their places in the history of our country, dark though they may be. Yet, it can't be denied that these people, these outsiders, are very much American. While some of them did what they did out of some deranged sense of personal purpose, others acted out of a misguided love for their country and a concern that somehow things had gone awry, and only their actions could set things right. They held views and beliefs outside the current norm. They were the odd men out. They were misfits.

And is there anything more American than a misfit? Early on I pointed out that we're a country born of misfits, people seeking a new home. When you get down to the bare bones of it, we're nothing more than a country of misfits. That is how America got its start, as a nation of misfits, people with beliefs contrary to the norm, looking for a place to belong and looking to find their place in the world.

As these thoughts crossed my mind, there onstage right before me, not more than a few feet away, Danny Borneo of the *Old City Sideshow* out of Philadelphia jutted his head into a shower of sparks coming off a metal grinder worked by Martin Ling. His eyes only protected by goggles, he thrust every inch of his face into a glorious arc of vibrant reds, golds, and oranges, striking his flesh and flaring in the air, a fireworks display gone terribly wrong. Now if that ain't a misfit, I don't know what is.

Danny is part of a larger American tradition of sideshow misfits that is seeing a rare but new birth, part of the very tradition that Sideshow School sought to keep alive. I wondered how many others were out there attempting to keep these traditions alive, and, more importantly, how many more I could possibly see in a short amount of time. *Sideshow Gathering* certainly helped bring some of the talent and misfits to me, but first I began in Washington, DC.

When I first visited the Palace of Wonders in Washington, DC, I was clueless. I had absolutely no context whatsoever. At the time, I had no idea that Thrill Kill Jill designed the *Palace of Wonders* and no idea that author/publisher and former co-owner of the American Dime Museum, James Taylor, housed a museum of bizarre items on the upper floor. When I arrived I expected to see a simple theater, possibly a bar wrapped around a performance space. What I encountered was so much more.

The *Palace of Wonders* is housed in a building that seems wedged into a strip of dismal, dark, and dingy buildings in the northeast section of the DC area. Driving along, there's clearly no doubt whatsoever which building belongs to the *Palace*. It stands out like a sore thumb, brightly colored sideshow banners beckoning passersby with wonders such as the Fiji Mermaid and a Living Unicorn, the ancillary sign, jutting from the front of the building exclaiming PALACE OF WONDERS, with brightly lit bulbs flashing around it.

The inside, I discover, is even more captivating than the outside, with not only signs, banners, and other ephemera littering the place but numerous magazine and newspaper articles about performers past and present lining the walls. I find one about Melvin Burkhart, right near the stage, with a picture of him hammering that oh so large nail into his head, a smile forever on his face.

The front of the *Palace* is lined with a bar that leads up to a modest stage for performers. There's a set of stairs that leads to the second floor. On your way up, behind glass, is a replica of the Elephant Man seated and dressed in a dapper suit, and on the second floor are all manner of bizarre items such as two-headed goats, multiheaded animals, and skulls galore. But it's not the museum that drew me there, but, rather, one of the acts that performs there—*The Cheeky Monkey Sideshow*.

The brainchild of Stephon Walker, *The Cheeky Monkey Sideshow* is, by all accounts, a modern-day sideshow that performs in theaters, performance spaces, and private functions. Anywhere there's a sideshow need, they're there.

Stephon started his career as an actor, seeking out parts to play at the age of seventeen, then through the course of acting started performing magic. Eventually, he found his way to the sideshow.

One of the main facets of the sideshow throughout the 1990s was the *Jim Rose Circus Sideshow*, which presented sideshow stunts and skills cloaked in gore, shock, and awe all wrapped around various forms of rock and metal music. Stephon pointed out that while he never saw the Jim Rose show, he saw many people at the time who were trying to do a Jim Rose-type presentation.

"So, essentially all I saw was college-age, tattoo-covered people being as gross as they could with heavy metal music in the background."

It didn't leave much of an impression. Then he caught an episode of *Penn & Teller's Sin City Spectacular* in which Todd Robbins was performing, and everything changed.

"He had a completely different approach and that sparked an interest."

Using his acting background as a hook and a bit of a crutch, he felt his way into the performance of sideshow stunts and skills was through something that would be heavily character based.

"Once the character was set, the first two or three routines came quickly based on that character."

The character he came up with was Swami Yomahmi. Originally toying with a play on the word geek, which was an old sideshow routine wherein a performer bites the heads off live animals, Stephon sought to make his character a nerdy, geeky misfit. Wearing a turban, bow tie and bowling shoes, everything organically grew from the character he created.

"I wanted everything to be motivated. I didn't want it to be here's the stunt, okay, I'm going to do the stunt, now the stunt's over."

He spent six years successfully honing the character and the stunts the Swami performed wherever he could, finding a home and seasonal performance place at the *Maryland Renaissance Faire*, though he was interested in performing for a formal sideshow.

"I wanted to get involved in a sideshow troupe, but that would have involved traveling, and my son was only five at the time."

Instead, he invoked the Nike mantra of "Just Do It" and decided to create his own show, and thus was *The Cheeky Monkey*

Sideshow born. In addition to Swami Yomahmi, the Cheeky Monkeys are rounded out with a true variety of other acts that include Mr. Eon, who brings a magic and mentalism facet to the show, and Damien Blade, who swallows swords and at times does so while juggling,

There's also Trinket, who performs an Indian Sword Basket routine (in lieu of and in the tradition of the blade box routine). However, what's unusual about Trinket, and what makes her unique in the realm of the sideshow performers that I've already seen presenting the blade box and like routines, is that she is a true contortionist. Others stretch and seem to bend their bodies before entering the blade box, but Trinket is the real deal. In addition to stuffing herself into the Indian Sword Basket, she also forces her entire body through a plastic hanger as well as a tennis racquet—a junior-sized racquet at that.

Sally the Cinch is their anatomical wonder. She dresses as a belly dancer, but doesn't dance. Rather, she uses the outfit to highlight her midsection so that all is clearly visible when she wraps a black leather belt around her body. She then uses the belt to cinch down her belly to a mere twelve inches.

There's Sensoriel, their fire performer, who not only eats fire but also infuses an exotic dance using large fans of flames, the heat of which the audience can feel wafting off the stage, and Mab, Just Mab, who performs a variety of acts including a straitjacket escape, glass walking, the bed of nails, and tunes on the ukulele at times. Finally, there's Calibano, their animal oddity that's billed as "the beast that walks like a man."

Each member of the group seems to follow the standards set by Stephon for his own character, infusing and bringing not only more than just stunts to the stage, but, rather, fully fleshed out characters and routines that bring the entertainment level even higher.

"I stopped doing magic because so many performers were focused on the trick and not the presentation or the entertainment value," Stephon said. "And if you can't entertain your audience, you're just masturbating. Anyone who's a performer is stroking his ego. You don't do this unless you want affirmation from an audience that you're a good person and good performer. However, there's got to be a dividing line between letting your audience stroke your ego and you stroking your ego in front of the audience."

The same is true for the sideshow duo out of Michigan, Knotty Bits, that is made up of Gwyd the Unusual and his partner Sylver Fyre. Steeped in a magic background that found them doing more gore-and-blood-based magic shows, they slowly made their way into the world of the sideshow by adding fire-eating into their acts.

"We got approached by someone who said, 'You should come perform at our venue doing a fire show,'" Gwyd said. "And I asked, 'How long would that be?' And they said a half hour to forty-five minutes. And I thought about it. A half hour to forty-five minutes of fire; they're going to go to sleep."

So they fleshed out a few other routines utilizing some of the other sideshow skills they'd picked up from here and there, with an eye on humor and presentation.

"So we said, 'What can we do for the last half hour or forty minutes based on what we have?' I thought I could do magic, we could do this, or she could dance. But then we were like, well, we have all these sideshow skills, so why don't we just do a sideshow?"

"The skills we kind of learned along the way," Sylver added. "We didn't have the luxury of going to a school, so we kind of picked them up as we went from some people we knew."

"If we wanted to learn glass walking we went to a glass walker," Gwyd said. "The way we developed the show is because the venues that we do are very family oriented, we don't do the big, bloody, Jim Rose type of show."

"Which is very opposite of how we started as performers," Sylver noted.

Gwyd agreed. "We wanted to do a show that I could bring my kids to. And they come to them now and they think it's the greatest thing. So it's very important to be more humorous than out and out in your face gore."

For them, the stunts were always second to the presentation. And in the vein of keeping everything family-friendly, they increased the amount of humor and toned down if not entirely excised any horror, gore, and extreme shock-value pieces from the show. While they still offer it should a client want a show like that, they have an eye to keeping everything on a level that will play to almost any audience, which has seen an increase in the number of shows they've gotten.

The *Olde City Sideshow* can mostly say the same given their penchant for the traditional, classic style of sideshow they present. Having grown out of Philadelphia, *The Olde City Sideshow* is composed of three members: Martin Ling the Suicide King, Reggie Bügmüncher, and Danny Bornero; however, *Olde City* started out as just two of them, Martin and Danny.

"Danny went and learned a lot of the acts from Todd Robbins and came back to me," Martin recalls. "And I have theatrical experiences. I work in the theater industry, and we sort of sat down and said this whole neoburlesque scene is really big, and at one time that was a sideshow act, so why not ride on the coattails of that and sort of form a little sideshow troupe ourselves. And at that time it was just the two of us. And we were discussing what acts we could do, what we could bring back, and how we wanted to go about doing it, and one of the first things we decided was that we wanted to do a classical show, as opposed to some of the newer stuff like Jim Rose. There are a lot of blood shows and gross-out shows, but we wanted to bring back the traditional, classical art from the earlier day and age."

"Or what people would think would be classical," Danny points out. "Actual old-time sideshow presentations, they're great. And as a performer I enjoy watching it, but a lot of people are very bored by it because it's just a grind of one act after another."

One of the things Martin and Danny figured out early on was the fact that they wanted a talker as part of their act. Being that, at that point, there were at least two of them with a variety of skills, having a talker, or someone who acts as a sort of narrator made sense, freeing each of them to focus and concentrate on their own individual performances.

"The talker is one of the most important parts of the sideshow," Mike Vitka said. An alumni of my Sideshow School class, Vitka and I took two different paths following the class. While I set out to write a book, Vitka contacted Ward Hall and Chris M. Christ of *Hall & Christ's World of Wonders*, one of the few traveling carnival sideshows left in the United States. During classes one day our instructor was asked whether there were any traveling sideshows left, and he referred us to the *World of Wonders*, providing the number for anyone interested.

"I don't think he thought I was going to call," Vitka recalled. "Well, I remember he was going to call up Chris, because I asked him if there was any of this still going on, and he took my phone because his wasn't working and they talked for fifteen minutes and didn't mention that there was somebody who wanted to do the sideshow. So on the subway back to where I was staying, I called the number myself and talked to Chris, and he said to send some pictures. So I sent him some pictures and told him I wanted to do the show. Then it was on Easter Sunday I was asleep and got a phone call that woke me up. 'This is Ward Hall,' Ward said in his wavering voice, 'and we'd like you to come to the Meadowlands....' He then went through the show, telling me that they had a four-legged girl, and this illusion and that illusion. He named all the illusions and what they had for the show."

Just coming off Sideshow School, Vitka had few skills under his belt, so he was trained in the art of talking on the bally stage. It's the talker's job not only to gather a crowd (sometimes called a tip) but also to turn that crowd into paying customers who'll purchase a ticket to the show. All of which is not nearly as easy as it seems.

"What they gave me was stock phrases they've been using since the beginning of time. And when I went up there, it was such confusion because I was getting direction on it from both Ward and Chris, and they both have such different methods on talking, and then Tommy who'd done it for a couple years gave me some of the best advice, and really helped streamline what everyone was saying. And right as I was starting, Red Stuart came by and gave me his advice. So I got a lot of good instruction from a lot of different sources on it and ultimately became very good at it."

Vitka worked for *World of Wonders* for two seasons, and learned a lot about not only talking outside on the bally stage but also talking the different exhibits and acts inside the show as well. When you think about this position, when you consider what they're doing, you realize it has more to do with being a salesman than being an actor, since your goal is exactly that: not only are you selling the audience on buying a ticket, but you're selling them on what they're seeing if you're working inside the show. You're selling them the fiction that sideshows sometimes present as truth.

"You just have to believe what you're saying," Vitka said with a bit of a wry smile on his face. "Once you get the crowd interested, you've got them. You've got to choose who in the crowd you're going to pick on first, and you get that person in, then someone will follow them, then they'll go in and others will follow. Soon the whole crowd's buying a ticket. It's all psychology, and the important thing is to think of it like you're selling it to them. There was one person who this past summer was with them, and they tried him on the bally and it didn't work out because he was approaching it like it was a theater performance. He was performing rather than selling the show. You've got to sell them on these strange things, and you've got to sell them the tickets. It's like salesmanship, and this other guy was doing it like it was a stage play, which sounded really good, but no one was buying it because he was performing and not being real about it, and then the crowd will go in and is going to find out that it wasn't real at all, but they believed it going in. You have to *make them believe*. Even the ones who know it's going to be fake, you have to sell them on it, and help them suspend their disbelief. They have to think 'well, maybe, this will be something.' "

Vitka found working inside the tent no easier. Illusions in the sideshow have been a staple for many years. With the Gorilla-to-Girl illusion, the crowd sees a gorilla transform into a woman and vice versa before their very eyes being one of the ones seen most often. Another might include the Snake Girl, which appears to be a full-bodied python with the head of a woman.

"When I worked on the inside, people at first *hated* the illusions, because there was nothing good about them. It was like throwing the curtain back, and it's an awful falling apart thing with some bored girl in it. But when I did the Snake Girl, I had to do something, and it was right around the time that, this past summer, on the news people thought they'd found the real Bigfoot. And this was that same weekend that I was talking about the Snake Girl, and instead I didn't talk about the Snake Girl, I started talking about Bigfoot. I went out there and I said, 'Have you heard on the news about that thing they found? The Bigfoot, the Sasquatch. You've all heard about that. The missing link between man and ape.' And the audience was like yeah, I've seen it. At least one person in every crowd would say, 'I've heard about it, I've seen the Sasquatch, I saw it on the news.' And I would tell them 'Well, tonight you're not going to see the Sasquatch, you're not going to see the missing link between man and ape, TONIGHT YOU'RE GOING TO SEE THE MISSING LINK BETWEEN MAN AND SNAKE!' At that, I'd throw back the curtain, and more often than not, they appreciated it. They were rapt in attention because they were able to connect it to something that was actually currently happening. And they were misdirected, because they thought they were going to see something that wasn't there."

For the traveling sideshow, sideshows that existed on traveling from town to town and to city to city in the early part of the twentieth century, the talker was exceedingly important since that was the show's first contact with the paying customer. The talker was the one who would quite literally talk the crowd out of their hard-earned money, convincing them to hand it over to the sideshow rather than, say, a concession stand or someplace else on the midway.

However, with groups like the *Olde City Sideshow*, the importance of the talker comes into question since they weren't necessarily working on a midway where it was necessary to draw the customers into the show. But in structuring their show in a classic and traditional manner, *Olde City* felt the position of talker was important, guiding the audience through the show as a narrator and lifting the burden of each act presenting its own script. It streamlined the show while at the same time it gave it the anchor to the past for which they were looking.

"We had a clear-cut idea as to how we wanted the show to go," Danny said. "A lot of people talk their acts, but we find that we're doing so much stuff onstage, we thought it smart to have a talker. Also, talking is a skill and an act all its own."

With a mixed bag of skills between them, from sword-swallowing to fire-eating to the human blockhead to other stunts, it seemed they might be a strong act with just the two of them, but then Reggie Bügmüncher approached them.

"Reggie came to me," Danny recalled, "and said, 'I want to be in the sideshow. What can I do?' And I was like, well, if she wants to do it, let me give her something heinous to do and if she'll do it, then cool. So, I said, 'All right, eat bugs.'"

"I needed a creative outlet," Reggie said, "and was really

interested in what they were doing. So when Dan said, 'Eat bugs,' I said, 'Done.' I used to work at a bait and tackle shop, so there was nothing that was really going to freak me out."

In addition to a well-honed contortion act that sees Reggie gliding her body through a tennis racquet and doing a bed of nails routine, Reggie became the *Olde City Sideshow*'s insectivore, eating live bugs before a live audience.

"I do enjoy doing it. When people enjoy watching me do it, I enjoy doing it a lot more; when people don't enjoy it, then it's more of an act of defiance where angry Reggie comes out. Usually, it's kind Reggie onstage."

"It's ironic," Martin noted, "since she was a vegan for quite a long time in her life. The first time when she ate worms was in my kitchen. She discovered that she can't chew the worms, they fought her back."

Reggie agreed. "The crickets I chew because they're feisty. The mealworms I chew because it kind of grosses people out, but other worms I don't. And the fish I don't, I just swallow them whole. The worms, if you catch them at the wrong moment, they coil up, and then they're really hard to get through. I think that part of the act is looking like it's enjoyable and carefree. If I sit there and gnash at what's in my mouth, then it looks like I'm fighting the worm, and I don't want to have an angry character."

Ultimately, it was the style of show that Martin and Danny were creating and forming that not only attracted Reggie to them but kept her with them.

"I like that we do a traditional show, and I like that we make people happy, that they walk away with a kind of sense of wonder that you really don't see a lot in the sideshow. In a lot of shows, people walk away either confused or grossed out. People walk away from us with a sparkle in their eyes, and they're excited about it, like when you're little and you'd go see something amazing."

And while they learned from experienced performers like

Todd Robbins and Harley Newman, there was no end to what they learned simply by performing. Take, for example, the story of "The Fish That Lived."

"We did this music festival," Reggie recalled. "There was this period of time when we got asked to do a lot of benefits. And this was a cystic fibrosis benefit. And when we show up, we found out we weren't performing on the stage, we were performing in the parking lot on the asphalt, and each of our acts would take place in between bands. So we had to break up a set. So it was like two or three acts in between bands."

After they'd arrived and found out the performance situation, they then realized that the audience wasn't what they'd expected either. "It was a kind of well-to-do area, and not really the people that were out for a sideshow."

At this point they considered a few new spins for the contortion act, and thought of possibly stuffing Reggie into something small and bringing her out in it. "We'd been working on the contortion act, and we'd tried a couple of trunks, but they didn't work out, so we found this huge Rubbermaid container that I fit into, but unfortunately it was clear at the bottom. The night before the show, Dan drilled some holes in it so I could breathe, and it was my first time actually staying in the container for an extended period of time, and I'm not really claustrophobic, but I was really afraid of the position I was in while in the container. So I said, 'Do not drop this, guys, I will break my neck.'

"So I was going to hide behind stage for a while. [Then] they were going to carry it out, and they had a tarp covering it so that you couldn't see me in the bottom because it was clear. And they get right out to where I'm to start performing in this parking lot filled with people, and all of a sudden I hear a BANG, and next thing I know I'm sprawled out on the parking lot. The entire bottom half of the thing had fallen out under my weight. And the audience? There's no concern, there's no laughter, there's no anything. And I was like, 'Ta-da.'

"I pick myself up from the tarp and I sit down and start doing the insectivore act, and it was when I did crickets and mealworms and a bunch of other stuff, and I get to the goldfish.

"Now, the backstory to the goldfish is that I get peer pressured at the store to buy a bigger one than I normally would swallow. Because I go in there at the last minute and I ask for this goldfish and she pulls it out in the container. She asks, 'Is this good?' And she's getting ready to pour it in the bag, and I say, 'You know it's a little bit too big, could I get a different goldfish?' And she asks, 'What size tank is it going in?' And I had this idiot moment where I say, 'This size tank right here'"—rubbing her stomach—"and I did it in a creepy voice, and she said, 'You're not going to eat the fucking goldfish.' And I was like, 'Bad joke?' And she said, 'Damn right!' and hands me the bag.

"So I bring it out to the show, and Dan says, 'That's a big fish,' and I said, 'Yeah, it's cool. I'll do it.' I go to get it down because it took several swallows, the dorsal fin cut my throat, so I finally get it into my throat and I can feel it moving. And Dan said he could see my shoulders twitching and I was fighting it, and I lifted my head and coughed and this goldfish shoots right out of my throat, lands directly back in the now empty glass, and it's flopping.

"The audience isn't moving. There's not a smile. You could hear crickets chirping behind the amps, and from the back of the crowd this kid says, 'For the love of god put some water in the glass,' and Dan does and the fish starts swimming around like nothing happened."

That's the story of the fish that lived.

What's been truly fascinating has been the way in which science has come into play with many sideshow acts, the relationship between physics and the bed of nails for instance or a subtle fact about the anatomy that allows one to slide a nail into his nose. Surprisingly, Reggie has a similar, esoteric fact along these lines with regard to her insectivore act.

"That act has not always worked out well for me. It's how I discovered I have a fatal shellfish allergy. I was eating crickets, mealworms, night crawlers, and goldfish. Initially it was the crickets. Crickets, mealworms, and cockroaches have the same protein as shellfish.

"We had done a walk-around at a show, and I was eating crickets in a corner in front of everybody, and I started getting itchy and breaking out. And it was only my second or third walk-around show, and Martin's says, 'Oh, you're just nervous, don't worry about it.' And I was like, 'I feel woozy.' And Martin says 'You're fine.' So I actually made it through the whole show, but I was bright red. I make it over to a friend at the end of the show and say, 'Take me outside,' and as I'm holding on to her, I can barely stand and my vision goes. And I was like I can't see and my hearing is going in and out and I don't know what's happening. And I throw up, and the whole goldfish comes out and it has black eyes.

"I need to go to the hospital, and I didn't have health insurance at the time, so I was really afraid. Because what I was holding out for was that it'd get either really bad or go away, and if it got really bad, I'd go to the hospital. So finally I said, 'Call 911.'

"The ambulance arrives and they ask Dan, 'So, what, she ate a bug?' And Dan says, 'Dude, she ate a *lot* of bugs.' So at this point the EMTs are wondering what the hell was going on and Dan tries to explain, 'You know, we're in a sideshow, and she does this insectivore act.'

"The EMTs come over and at this point my throat's starting to close and my lips are spread across my face, and the guy leans over and immediately starts giving me intravenous epinephrine.

"I thought it was just the crickets. I did mealworms, but that time I had an Epi Pen."

While there is certainly no limit to the number of people who are willing to chow down on bugs and other assorted insects before a live audience, another, and probably one of the youngest performers around, is Brett Loudermilk. Loudermilk also comes from quite an unusual background.

"Growing up, I was raised in a Pentecostal tent show. My grandfather was a Pentecostal preacher, faith healer, he did all this crazy shit while at the same time being an atheist con man. From the time I was born until about the age of five, I grew up in this, and I remember how loud it was, how bizarre it was with people speaking in tongues.

"My grandfather would be up there, and he had this one line I remember clear as day. He'd be talking to the congregation and he'd bellow out, 'Give me *alllllll* your money!' Not *some* of it. Don't give him *10 percent*. Give me *all* of your damn money! And they would, these poor people."

Given his grandfather's shortcomings, Loudermilk portrays him as an "ethical con man."

"He hired actors to travel with the show.... He would never ever heal anyone that was clearly sick. He did the leg lengthening and shortening. He did all of it. The poison drinking, it was hard-core Appalachian mountain Pentecostal revivals. And one day, all these sick people following him from show to show to show, he couldn't take it anymore, and he came out to his congregation, said he was an atheist, told them they should look into it, and sold his tent to a preacher friend of his. So that's how I grew up. I got this con man in my blood and this showmanship, and I've always been a performer.

That said, Loudermilk found an interest in the sideshow at an extremely young age, having hammered his first nail into his head at the age of eight.

"I built my first bed of nails when I was like ten or eleven with my grandfather, but I started when I was eight. I ham-

mered a nail up my nose when I was eight years old. I was
living in North Carolina, and we'd just moved from Winston-
Salem to Charlotte, and the year before I had seen Bobby
Reynolds' show *Reynolds Believe It You're Nuts*. It was a museum show. And being six or seven at the time, looking up
at the giant banner line...I'd heard about sideshows, and I
think the year before I saw some grind shows, but nobody
would let me go in.

"So I see this giant banner line, and I beg my mother for
the two bucks to let me go in. And I'm so excited that I pay
my money and run straight in, and I didn't get my ticket so
they didn't tear my ticket. And the guy at the ticket booth,
at the time it seemed like it was twelve feet tall, this giant
ticket booth, a horrible-looking scary carny with a giant top
hat, is yelling at me for my ticket and I'm freaking out looking for my ticket. So I run over and get my ticket and walk
in and it's a bunch of *shit*.

"I walk around the tent and I see the Fiji mermaid, and I
looked at it, and that really stuck with me. And I read the
title, and I remember hearing about it before. Then I went
down the line, and there was chupacabra roadkill.

"So I'm looking at all this stuff, and I'm feeling like I got
ripped off, but at the same time there's this tingling in me
and I think, 'Wow this is really cool!' So I left and I kind of
forgot about it.

"And then, working at a *Renaissance Faire*, I lied to the production staff and told them that I was twelve so that I could
volunteer there without a parent. They must have been the
most irresponsible production department in the world. I
don't look twelve now!

"I was a very mousy little kid, but I got in, and I was working as a hawker/cryer and stagehand at one of the stages, and
there's a man named Dexter Tripp, and he's a juggler/
tightrope walker on the *Ren Faire* circuit, he does absolutely
amazing stuff. He walks up an inclined rope while it's on fire.

"I begged and begged Dexter to teach me something. And it's between shows, we're backstage, and I asked him for the ten thousandth time, I asked him to teach me something. He walks into his trailer and gets a nail. He hands it to me, tells me to lick it off, and shove it up my nose. Didn't start with a Q-tip! Eight years old, 16 p. nail, right up the nose. Thank god I've got big sinuses. It took about a half hour, I sneezed a lot, but I got it up there, and he said, 'Now you're a human blockhead.'"

That's when Loudermilk really got the bug for sideshow stunts and the like. "Variety acts in general have always really grabbed me, and in meeting Dexter I thought, 'This is it.' One of the main reasons I do what I do is because I'm keeping it alive. The history is something that I absolutely adore. I love it. And Dexter just turned me on to this weird world. And through Dexter I learned how to eat fire, walk on broken glass, and a few of the things I taught myself."

In his off time, Loudermilk also delved into the crafts of welding and jewelry making, which ultimately led to a melding of two arts.

"I started learning all I could about glass, all I could about welding, jewelry making, all that stuff, and I had heard about the Human Lighthouse act, which is, basically, you put the light in your nose, and you've got a watch glass in your mouth, and it lights up. And then Nippullini started making nails. And I thought, 'I wish I could make my own nail,' and thought a glass nail would be cool. And I knew Pyrex conducts light, because when I have pieces in the fire, the ends of them are as bright as the fire is. So I make my first nail, I shove it in my nose, and it's so smooth, it just goes right in, then it hits me, 'Wait, I have to get a flashlight.' So I run out of my studio area, grab a flashlight, run into the bathroom, turn the lights off, shove the flashlight in my mouth, and the head of the nail lights up."

With the desire to be a sideshow performer burning in

him, and with many of the basic skills already under his belt, it seemed time to tackle the one act he'd attempted a few times and still was unable to succeed at.

"I learned how to sword-swallow in two weeks. Coat hanger, coat hanger, coat hanger, then, *bam*, a sword. I was doing it twenty times a day. For years I had the information in my head, I knew what to do, I just didn't have the impetus. I tried doing it, but just couldn't do it. I called Todd [Robbins], and he said, 'Just do it. You can do it. You're a sideshow performer. Go all the way. If you're going to do this for a living, you need to be one of the few that can do this.' So I did it, and it took me two weeks, and at that point I was still in high school."

In addition to the occasional advice, Robbins also allowed Loudermilk the freedom to try some of the routines that had worked for him in the past, such as his cockroach routine.

I have been a flea circus proprietor for several years now—you've not lived until you've seen a flea walk the high wire, dive into a tiny pool of water, or get shot out of a cannon—I know more than a few odd little facts about bugs, and the one that Loudermilk takes advantage of in his act I became aware of at an early age.

Now given, I was a strange child. I must have been. I certainly don't have enough objectivity in my retrospective analysis of my youth, but I'm sure I was. I must have been. Why else would I play with ants?

Don't get carried away. Surprisingly, I never did use a magnifying glass while playing with ants. Rather, I had a small box, the kind you might get if you'd purchased a pair of earrings as a gift for your mother, say. And what I'd do is take the ants, put a few of them in this box, and then put the box in the freezer. What would happen next is not what you'd think.

No, it did not involve my mother beating my ass, nor did

it involve the ants ending up as a unique spice in either my father's or my sisters' meals. Though, if they did, I'd never tell. Rather, what I'd do after the box had been in the freezer a sufficient amount of time is bring it out into the warmth of the summer day and remove the lid. What you'd find are the ants curled up in little balls, but, slowly but surely, as the sun warmed them, they'd wake up.

Ants, like many other creatures in the animal kingdom, go into a kind of hibernation during the winter and, of course, when the temperature goes down to a certain degree. Once warmed up again, the ants would resume their natural lives, scurrying from the box and going about their merry ways. Assuming I hadn't casually dropped them into a pot of spaghetti sauce while they'd been on ice. But this isn't a confession. I'm pleading the fifth. Okay, I did it once. Don't tell anyone. With that bit of information, let's return to Loudermilk's tale.

"I can throat things," Loudermilk continued. "And Todd gave me the act that he's not done in years, which is swallowing and regurgitating cockroaches.

"So I take out six cockroaches on ice, and I bring somebody up onstage. Now, Todd just did the cockroaches, he never ate bugs, and I do the bug eating. So in my routine I say, 'I'm not about grossing people out, if I wanted to gross you out, I'd take these night crawlers, if it wouldn't make you sick I'd take them and I'd eat them.' And then I eat some. 'But no, I don't want to do that. I don't want to gross you out too much. If I really, really wanted to gross you out, I'd take these maggots,' and then I shovel them in my mouth and say, 'But no I don't want to gross you out. But really, if I wanted to make you roll in the aisles because I'd done something despicable, I'd take these cockroaches...' Then I take the container, put it down, take the cloth off, there's six of them all on ice, and they're not moving.

"I get a woman onstage to pick one of them out, and I explain the cockroaches are on ice. They are alive, but they're asleep basically, and I let her pick one out, and try to get her to do it with her bare hands. I pick it up, put it in my mouth, swallow it. I take a magnifying glass and a flashlight and go around the front few rows and show that my mouth is empty, and then go back up onstage. By this time my body has heated up the cockroach enough that it's alive and well. I bring it up, if I can. Sometimes when I keep it down, I lose it and have to do it again. I bring it up, and I let it crawl out onto my face and put it back with its friends and put it away. It's pretty *and* disgusting."

It's a given that Loudermilk, while young, has learned some amazing feats. The skills are clearly present, allowing him to amaze audiences with his sword swallowing, blockhead, and other acts. He still works on his presentations, utilizing any venue to hone his routines so that they work in tandem with the stunt he is performing.

It seems that, today, in the twenty-first century, the sideshow is alive and well, but has evolved into something much different from what it was during the time when Barnum first gathered these acts together under one tent, or even in the early part of the twentieth century when sideshows were connected with carnivals. Carny Sideshows: Weird Wonders of the Midway? The title is a bit of a misnomer. Feats such as the ones I learned at Sideshow School may have found homes alongside the carnival or on the midway at one time, but finding them there now, well, they're few and far between.

Instead, today's performers seek out theaters and performance spaces in which to ply their trades, bringing something new and fresh and different to these strange acts but, at the same time, continuing a tradition handed down from one performer to the next. And now more than ever, given the venues in which they're now performing, from the more experienced to those that are more green, the importance and strength of any act lies not so much in *what* you're doing, but *how* you do it.

The question really comes down to this: as Stephen Walker put it, do you want to have the audience stroke your ego, or do *you* want to stroke your ego in front of the audience?

CHAPTER TWELVE

~⌣~

GRADUATION
CEREMONY AND EGRESS

Do not go where the path may lead; go instead
where there is no path and leave a trail.
—Ralph Waldo Emerson

Some men see things as they are and ask why.
Others dream things that never were and ask
why not.
—George Bernard Shaw

At Sideshow School there is no diploma. You don't get anything stating you've completed the course, nothing scrawled on sheepskin, onion paper, or the scaly flesh of a mermaid—though the last one would be apropos.

Instead, we're asked to stand onstage in a straight line, facing the bleachers where the audience sits. There is only one person sitting on the bleachers, and that's our instructor. We're asked to stand with our torches lit, and one by one we pass along the line the bottle of fuel, and one by one we each take a deep swig of it. This is the Sideshow School Commencement Exercise.

When all of our mouths are full, we breath fire as one, six of us blasting forth from the stage as deeply and as full as we can, the balls of fire meeting some three feet before us, culminating in a heat that distorts the vision and fills the room with the sweet, pungent scent of fire, smoke, and fuel. Much like the week and the experiences of learning the many and varied skills of the sideshow, the heat from the fireballs remains long after the actual flames have dissipated.

After we're finished and give our thanks to our instructor, some of the class head up to the boardwalk for beer and clams. Others head for the subway, which can be easily seen some blocks away, as in this section of Brooklyn they are elevated.

I head down to the beach. My wife and son are waiting for me at home, but I head down to the beach—if only for a few moments—to let the experiences wash over me. The week has been quick, too quick, and only the most foolish among us would believe that the graduation ceremony was an ending. Rather, it was a beginning.

But as my feet hit the beach, a beach that I've always considered so unlike the other beaches I've known in my life, more gritty and dirty than other beaches, I turn back and take in the strip of stores and arcades on the boardwalk. Some are still closed for the season and others are closed for good. Coney Island is a city in flux.

I turn back to the sea and, like Mozart haunted by his father in Peter Shaffer's *Amadeus*, my thoughts turn to my father as I consider the final reason I attended Sideshow School in the first place.

Three memories abound, none of them had to do with that day my parents took me to the circus and I'd gotten my first glimpse of the sideshow; no, these memories had nothing to do with the circus or the sideshow or performing.

The first comes from my childhood. I was six years old or possibly younger. My mother and I were in our basement where she was putting in a load of laundry while at the same time trying to organize and clean up the clutter that had accumulated from various projects my father had started.

"He starts things and never finishes them," she exclaimed. Evidence of this being true surrounded us. There was no denying it.

Years later, my father, who'd been born legally blind in his left eye, went for cataract surgery on his other eye. After the surgery, he was quite nearly completely blind until the eye healed, and, as he sat at the kitchen table one day during one of my visits, listening to the radio, we heard the announcer mention Robin Williams' vocal performance in the Disney film *Aladdin* as being stunning. My father, his hands wrapped around a cup of coffee before him, smiled.

"I'm hearing a lot about that movie," he said. "If the surgery is successful, I'd really like to see what it is everyone's talking about."

While the surgery was successful and he regained sight in his functioning eye, to the best of my knowledge a trip to see *Aladdin* never occurred.

Toward the end of his life, after he was diagnosed with cancer and lived for another nine months, slavishly going to chemotherapy and radiation treatments, he mentioned how he'd just like to get ahead of the game a bit with the disease to give my mother and him a chance to go down to Cape May, New Jersey, a final time. He put it off, and put it off, and put it off until his time was gone.

My greatest, most piercing memory of my father as I was growing up was of him coming home every night, and my mother asking him how his day was. His answer was always the same: "Same shit, different day."

I looked out at the ocean, and considered the things my father planned to do, the projects my father planned to finish, the things he wished he'd done, and the way in which, so often, he allowed them to slip through his fingers. Same shit, different day.

I'm no sideshow man.

But I love the sideshow.

I think it was this, more than anything that drove me to Sideshow School. It was this, more than any memory of a man standing onstage eating razor blades or of a man lying on a bed of nails. It was this, this need to do *something,* to wrap your hands, your heart, and your being around *something* that seemed out of reach, and to find out what you're truly capable of doing. To take every moment, every ridiculous idea, and act on them—because we only get to do all of this once. That, more than anything, is what drove me to Sideshow School. And this wasn't an end; this was a beginning. Once you realize your potential, once you see what it is that you can do, there is no limit to where you can take it.

I've lain on many beds of nails. I've put my hands in many animal traps, and stuck my tongue into mousetraps. I've driven nails into my nose and have poked, prodded, and continued to work on swallowing a sword. I headed home, and life went on. Today I occasionally play with fire, honing that skill.

And now, as I finish typing, I'm headed into my living room to shove something down my throat and see how far it goes. Nothing ever ends. Not until the day we die. Up to that point, we have nothing but time.

And potential.

SIDESHOW MENTORS, PERFORMERS, AND RESOURCES

Most, if not all, of the performers and shows mentioned in this book (including groups like the *Olde City Sideshow*, *Cheeky Monkey Sideshow*, and *Knotty Bits* among others) can be found and contacted easily via a quick Internet search. Most performers primarily work the areas in which they are based, but like any good sideshow performer, some will travel to where the jackpots can be found.

Following are a few of note, including info on Coney Island and Harley Newman, two resources for students seeking to learn the bizarre feats found in this book:

Todd Robbins
www.toddrobbins.com

Todd can be found at his website, as can information about where he's performing. If you've a chance to take in one of his shows, don't hesitate!

Coney Island USA
1208 Surf Avenue
Brooklyn, New York 11224
(718) 372-5159
www.coneyisland.com

Coney Island USA not only hosts a sideshow but is also host to Sideshow School and also offers a number of classes and events during the course of the year.

Harley Newman

www.bladewalker.com

harley@bladewalker.com

Harley Newman is a brilliant performer who for the past few years has offered a weekend class in sideshow skills. Contact him via e-mail, and if he's offering his class, go out of your way to take it.

James Taylor

www.shockedandamazed.com

James Taylor and his partners publish a number of just truly great books titled *Shocked and Amazed: On & Off the Midway*. If you're a lover of the sideshow, then they're books you won't want to miss. Check out their website for more info.

The Venice Beach Freakshow

909 Ocean Front Walk [the boardwalk]

Venice, CA 90291

(310) 314-1808

Sadly, I was unable to make it to the West Coast to take in what I've heard is an excellent museum show titled *The Venice Beach Freakshow*. All evidence and people I've spoken with have only the highest regard for this establishment, and I thought it wise to include it here.

Doug Higley

www.grindshow.com

doug@grindshow.com

Doug is a lover of the sideshow and a creator of the bizarre. Check out the books he has on his website as well as the assortment of ephemera he offers. Chills and thrills abound from this artist who's been grinding out this strange stuff since the 1970s.

Sideshow World

www.sideshowworld.com

Promoting the past and preserving the future, Sideshow World is the place on the Internet to go for information about the sideshow.

GLOSSARY OF CARNIVAL AND SIDESHOW TERMS AND LINGO

The following is a brief glossary of carnival and sideshow terms and lingo, compiled by Wayne N. Keyser for his website at *www.goodmagic.com*. Thanks to Wayne for allowing me to reprint part of his glossary here, and be sure to check out his site for even more info on the sideshow.

Alligator Man—Sideshow human oddity afflicted with a skin condition, commonly icthyosis, which gives the skin a scaly, reptilian appearance.

Amusement business—The trade magazine of the trade, originally *The Billboard*. Many traveling showmen would use *Billboard* as their address—the magazine would forward mail to them along the show's route.

Anatomical wonder—A sideshow performer able to do stunts such as "the man without a stomach" (pulling the gut in until the backbone shows), pulling themselves through a coat hanger or tennis racket, and other India Rubber Man stunts.

Baby show—Also known as *unborn, life, bottle, freak baby*, and *pickled punk show*.

Bally or ballyhoo—The *bally* is the "outside talker's" spiel drawing a crowd (called a "tip") to see a sideshow. The bally is a sophisticated commercial, usually illustrated with quick appearances by the performers featured in the show. Its longer, original form, ballyhoo, has come into general usage meaning "to attract the attention of customers/voters by raising a clamor." The word originated at the 1893 Columbian Exposition in Chicago, in the "Street of Cairo" pavilion. The performers from the Middle East spoke only Arabic. Exhibit manager W. O. Taylor would call the Beledi dancers (a term later corrupted, also by Taylor, to "belly dancers") and musicians out during slack periods to attract a crowd. Since these calls were on no set schedule, the tired performers would mutter "D'Allah hun," roughly meaning "Oh, for God's sake!," as they rose to the extra duty. Taylor began simply calling them to (as he heard it) *ballyhoo*. We do not know, though we can guess, what else the performers may have had to say about the boss in Arabic. The bally is also known as the *first opening*, while the inside talker would introduce the crowd to the show with the *second opening*. Ward Hall recently advised that the "most sure thing to draw a tip: (daytime) a beautiful girl in a revealing costume holding a big fat snake, (nighttime) fire-eating, fire juggling. To top this: A strong freak, such as a pinhead. But drawing a tip is just the start. Then you need to freeze the tip while the talker makes the pitch, and then to close the tip: a sword-swallower or fire blast. It must be instantaneous to close the bally. If you have a steady-moving large crowd, the bally should only last five or six minutes, and do six to ten ballys per hour. To entertain is not the purpose of the bally. It is to stop people so that you can sell the contents of the show. The entertainment is on the inside. The bally people, except the talker, should be called to the bally platform, and then all but the talker should leave while the talker brings the bally to its climax and turns the tip. To operate a strong bally show you need three or four people who only work the bally. There is no time for them to go inside and entertain. It is best to use three talkers to rotate, one hour on bally and two hours off. This way they will have the energy needed to punch hard for the hour they are on, when the show is playing spots where you get crowds from the time you open at 9 A.M. till closing at midnight or after, which is what a show needs to do if the operator expects to become wealthy. The most expensive thing you can have on the bally is an inexperienced, poor, lazy talker, which could cost you a fortune. The best talkers work on a percentage of the gross ticket sales to create the incentive to work hard when they are tired and would rather step down late at night, instead of making one more bally to get more gross. And of course give the talker one or more feature freaks to bear down on when they make the openings." Bally talkers often specialized, one talker making the opening and then handing the mike to another to make the pitch and turn the tip.

Banner—Canvas squares hung in front of sideshows depicting (usually in greatly exaggerated form) the wonders to be found inside. A single show would have a banner or two, a 10-in-1 would have a banner line in modular twelve-foot sections. Standard banner sizes were 8' x 10' or 10' x 12', with larger sizes, perhaps 14 or 16 feet, on the ends of a banner line. Banners spanning the attraction's doorway might be 36' x 8'. Taller doorway banners, perhaps 36' x 10', were tied off at an angle at the bottom, affording enough room for the crowd to walk under them.

Barker—*Barker* was never an authentic carnival term. Carnies call the person gathering a tip for a show a *talker*—the *outside talker* attracts the tip and the *inside talker* or *lecturer* conducts the crowd through a 10-in-1 show, describing the acts and building interest in the *blowoff*. Moreover, "hurry hurry hurry," the phrase you often hear chanted by the barker in movies, is far less sophisticated than the real outside talker's intricately contrived appeals. The term "barking" was in current use in mainstream culture in the early twentieth century to mean drawing customers by talking in a continual flow of repetitive lines and phrases. Barking was also called a *grind pitch* by some professional talkers. "Come on we got tomatoes today girls, a tisket a tasket, I sell them by the basket." Used primarily by vendors at a stationary spot, such as a vegetable stand or the doorway to a show (perhaps most recently heard from the doorways of Times Square sex shows). It's easy to see how the general public applied the term to the carnival talker. Differentiated from the *street cries* of vendors who traveled the street in wagons, whose cries tended to be more musical and more piercing in tone to attract the attention of people inside their houses.

Bed of nails—A common carny show stunt, and as with most such stunts (sword-swallowing, fire-eating, and the like), the secret is that there is no secret, you just do it. The usual bed of nails has so many nails set less than 1″ apart so that lying on them, though uncomfortable, does not puncture the skin. The average performer can safely allow an audience volunteer to stand on his chest while lying on the bed, and can allow a cinder block to be broken on his chest with a sledgehammer without ill effects (inertia keeps the shock wave within the cinder block, which isn't too hard to break).

Blade Box—An act in which the performer (usually a woman) lies in a box while steel blades are pushed through it, apparently a traditional "cutting a woman in half" illusion, until the blowoff is announced: "Sheila is going to step behind the curtain for a moment and remove her costume. We are not doing this to be lewd or crude, but this feat requires her to twist and contort her body so severely that she cannot perform it while hampered by even this small item of clothing (here, honey, just hand out that costume and I'll fold it up nice for you). And now that she has prepared herself, she will recline in the cabinet and (opening the curtain as Sheila, lying in the cabinet, waves her arm to the crowd) I'm going to close the lid. Notice that the lid has openings for thirteen steel blades (the crowd also notices even more openings they will get to peer through). Now I am not going to cut this beautiful young lady, because as I insert each blade she is bending, twisting, and contorting her body in and around every one of these blades of steel, just like a snake, just like a rubber band, she can bend her body as these blades threaten to sever the most delicate parts of her body. (Pause for a look down into the box.) And now I'm going to give the real men in the audience a chance to come up onstage and see for themselves! Sheila invites each and every one of you up here to see how she does it. You're going to see how her amazing body can twist around these razor-sharp blades; you're going to see the texture of her skin! But you should know that this lovely and talented little beauty receives no pay for displaying herself to your eyes in this fashion. Sheila feels that exposing her act and her body this way is worth one dollar, because she is paid only through your curiosity and your generosity. Now if I can get you all to line up at the foot of the stairs, just hand your dollar to the man at the foot of the steps and come up and see this beautiful little girl in the state she is in now, unashamed and waiting for you to view her." Of course, when you paid your dollar and looked into the box, the girl (who had so conspicuously handed out her garments) was wearing a tight bathing suit, and that's all that was promised; she's not wearing the costume you first saw her in. The tip was moved through the area so fast they hardly had a moment to figure out that they hadn't seen a nude girl, even though they had seen the "magic secret" of how she was contorted around the blades. A classic blowoff feature.

Blockhead act—An act in which a man *drives* a spike or nail into his nasal passage. Actually the spike inserts very easily, and the *hammering* is mimed.

Blowoff (sometimes shortened to "the blow")—This is where the real money is. Why? Because you don't have to split your *inside money* with the front office! At the end of a carnival show, the crowd (sometimes just the men) is often offered an extra added attraction for an extra fee. This is something either you can pay to see (if you've a strong enough stomach or perhaps a strong enough desire to see a lady you think might be naked, as implied with the blade box) or you could blow off and leave without seeing the extra feature. Since the inside talker was also usually the magician, he'd do his brief magic act for the ladies and children while the gents paid a little extra to go behind the curtain to see the blowoff. Always implied was the idea that the good stuff is in the attraction you haven't paid for yet. It might be simple to the point of crudity: "Okay boys, this is how it works.... Now that there's just us men in here, the tattooed lady is gonna go behind the curtain and any of you that wanna go with her can give me a dollar and follow along. She's gonna sit in a chair, she's gonna lift up her dress, and she's gonna show you what you've all been waiting to see. Now who's man enough to go back there and see for himself?" More often it was a bit more subtle: "Boys, we all know what you came here to see, and you've seen a good show already. I know there isn't a single one of you out there who doesn't think he already got his money's worth. But you came in here to see more than a set of knockers. And you're going to see A LOT MORE, I promise you. We couldn't tell you everything on the outside because you know there are women and kids on the midway. But back here we can talk right out. It's going to cost you another half a buck—but if it's the last fifty cents you have in the world, it'll be well spent. Lulu's going to put on a show you'll remember the rest of your days. And there ain't no fooling, neither. She's going to come out just the way you want her to, and you're gonna see it ALL!" It might even be possible to do a second ding after they've seen the lady naked: "Boys, us dancers, we don't get paid, only what we get in tips. Now I'm going to show you fellows something you may have heard about but I bet you ain't never seen it. And if you want to stay for it, why your tips will be the only pay I get. But it's worth it, believe me. You'll thank your lucky stars you did, and with what you'll learn tonight, when you go home you're going to make your own little ladies VERY happy they let you come in here! Let me give you a little hint. When I start this little private show just for you, there ain't going to be but two things on this stage, this soda bottle and me."

Bouncer—A rubber reproduction of a pickled punk. There were any number of reasons for using reproductions instead of genuine specimens including local legal restrictions and easier availability.

Cookhouse, Cookshack—Sometimes a large eating establishment open to the public, like a restaurant or cafeteria. More often, the place where personnel eat, not open to the public.

Dime museum—A collection of specimens, exotic objects and live acts and performances, usually set up in an old storefront. These were both the original museums and the original freak shows, most popular primarily in the nineteenth and early twentieth century. Present-day roadside museums are their descendants.

Ding—(1) The offering, to those customers already inside your show, of the chance to see a really special added attraction, not advertised on the outside, for an additional fee. The blade box illusion is a classic ding ("Come up and see how she fits in there for just a quarter—she couldn't do it if she had any clothes on."). (2) Expenses (over and above the percentage) paid to the carnival operator, such as charges for utilities, trash collection, insurance, sales tax, ID badges, parking space for your camper or trailer, another fee to park your car, security, inspection fees, advertising, official shirts, and tip to the lot manager. You might have to pay the operator's man to sell tickets, since they don't trust you. And, of course, they didn't tell you this in advance, nor did they tell you about the "pay one price for everything" promotion (so most of the crowd will be riding all day instead of buying tickets to your show). Somehow the operator's percentage, quoted to you as 50 percent of your gross, has mysteriously jumped to 57 percent, and the guy who told you 50 percent is nowhere to be found. And those "inside sales"? Not this time, unless you want to pay 57 percent of that money too. And on and on. You don't like it? Well, you're now blocked in by rides and trucks, and you're unable to leave.

Ding show—I remember going into an *absolutely free* show in Atlantic City in the 1960s. Inside, before getting to see "the real stuff," I was stopped at a gateway by the iron grip of the proprietor, saying, "Aren't you going to give a contribution?" No mention of what I was contributing to, but for a buck I got to see a series of cardboard dioramas depicting great naval actions, obtained free from the local Navy recruiting office. A Ding show is absolutely free, except that you aren't getting out without being strong-armed for a "contribution."

86'ed—Banned from the lot. The term is in general use meaning "we have no more (something)" or "to get rid of (something)." There are many folk etymologies explaining the origin of the term, but all are dubious.

Electric Chair act—An act (often called The Human Dynamo) in which the performer (usually named "Mister Electrico" or the like) would appear to be immune to the effects of electricity—actually a phenomenon of high-voltage electricity that permits an ungrounded person to light neon or fluorescent tubes at a touch and do other similar stunts without being harmed. The widespread availability of second-hand quack medical devices suitable for powering this phenomenon made it easy for carny electricians to rig the gaff, but this is a very dangerous stunt if done wrong. See Ray Bradbury's classic fantasy novel *Something Wicked This Way Comes* for a wonderful depiction of this act.

Freak show—A show where human oddities displayed themselves (often selling photos, Bibles, or other memorabilia). These were often 10-in-1 shows and usually featured born freaks, "made freaks" like tattooed people, and working acts like sword-swallowers and fire-eaters.

Gaff banner—A very attractive banner promising a world of wonders and a plethora of famous attractions...with cleverly worded bullets like Past and Present indicating that few (or none) of the attractions were actually there in the flesh. Photographs and other museum exhibits might show and tell you all about famous freaks.

Geek—An unskilled performer whose performance consists of shocking, repulsive, and repugnant acts. This "lowest of the low" member of the carny trade would commonly bite the head off a living chicken or sit in a bed of snakes. Some historians distinguish between geeks who pretend to be wild men and "glomming geeks" whose act includes eating disgusting things. See the 1949 movie *Nightmare Alley* for a good geek story as well as for an excellent depiction of the mentalist's technique of *cold reading*. In later years the geek show turned into a "see the pitiful victim of drug abuse" show. Geek as a verb (*he geeked*) is one of several terms in use among wrestlers meaning intentionally to cut oneself to draw blood.

Gibtown—Gibsonton, Florida, retirement spot (or winter quarters) for many show people. Pioneered by Jeannie (the half girl) and Al Tomaini (the giant), a married couple who retired from show business to open Giant's Camp restaurant and fishing camp there.

Girl in Fish Bowl ("Living Mermaid")—An illusion show: the viewer looks into the fish bowl (sometimes a lens, more often simply a dry mockup) to see a girl, often with a fish tail, apparently living underwater.

Girl-to-Gorilla show—An all-time moneymaker, this illusion show features a girl being changed (magically or scientifically) into a savage gorilla, which then "breaks out of its cage" frightening the crowd away. It uses a half-silvered mirror (one-way mirrors are not really one way, they just show whichever side is more brightly lit). There are variations on the theme, like skeleton-to-vampire or in older times, Galatea, after the myth of Pygmalion the sculptor and Galatea, the statue he brought to life. Simple upkeep and a little showmanship can make this show really frightening, but I have never seen it done with even the minimal care needed to arouse anything but disappointment. "Zambora, the ape girl, the ape girl, she's alive! Only the brave are invited to see the ape girl! She is locked in a solid steel cage for your protection, and under bright lights, you'll see the change begin: her forehead will begin to recede, her eyebrows will protrude, fangs will begin to grow in her mouth, and her clothes will fall away from her body! A heavy coat of hair will grow from every square inch of her skin, the long straggly hair of a gorilla!"

Grind—In the "outside talker's" spiel from a show front, the compelling and rhythmic verbal conclusion meant to move the patrons into the show. It differs from the opening bally, which is meant to get the attention of midway strollers and "build a tip," or sell them on the show they can see. Also means to stay in the joint and work even though there's almost no business.

Grind show—A show or attraction the customers can walk through and see at any time without being guided through. It has no bally, no beginning or end time; the front men and ticket sellers just "grind away" all day. Most of the shows on carnival midways today are grind shows, the grind blaring over the midway from an audiotape loop and sound system.

Human Pincushion—An act in which the performer sticks sharp objects into his flesh. Also known as fakirs, from the Indian term. The secret to this act (like the secret to many sideshow acts) is that there is no secret. Puncturing one's flesh is painful, but less so than the audience thinks. You can learn to tolerate the pain.

Jackpots—Troupers' tall tales (regular folks might say "war stories") of their former exploits. "Cutting up jackpots" is the expression given to swapping these stories.

Lobster Man—Human oddity with any of what are now called "limb reduction disorders," a birth defect giving their arms or legs or both the appearance of a lobster's claws.

Mark—A carnival term for a townsperson, in the sense of "victim." When a carny spotted a towny with a big bankroll, he would give him a friendly slap on the back, leaving a chalk mark so other carnies would know that this customer had lots of money. Often the ticket seller would mark the *mark*. The booth would have a high counter, above the average person's eyesight, and the ticket seller would short-change the customer, leaving the change on the counter. If the customer didn't notice or didn't count his change, the ticket seller would lean over to give him some friendly advice about the best attractions, putting his hand on the customer's shoulder to point him toward the show he simply must see, simultaneously dusting his back with chalk from a hidden supply. If the customer instead complained about the wrong change, the ticket seller could always push the remaining change to him and say, "I told you to take it." And what do you do when you spot a mark? You *play* him—that's right, just like you play a fish. But a carny truism is, "Always leave the mark a dollar for gas." With gas money he can go home (you don't want him stuck there growing angrier with you every minute).

Midway—There's no midway on a carnival. When games and sideshows were attached to a circus, the midway was the game and sideshow area between the main ticket booth and the entrance to the big top, literally midway between the two. You would often hear sideshow ballys claiming that "the big show doesn't start for forty-five minutes, there's plenty of time to see this entire exhibit." A carnival is really just a midway without an accompanying circus. The carnival lot, instead of being a straight alley leading from entrance to big top, is U-shaped, with the best locations on the right side as you enter, and the big rides and shows at the apex.

Nut—The "overhead," or operating expenses of a show or a joint (still used in the movie theater business as the "house nut"). Supposedly from the idea of creditors removing the nuts from wagon wheels and not returning them until paid. A show always seeks to make the nut and begin making a profit above expenses. A show that hadn't yet made the nut was said to be "on the nut" and one that had was said to be "off the nut." It was good if you could count on your show to always "carry the nut." Also "burr."

Pickled punks—A carny term, never used in front of the general public, describing deformed fetuses preserved in formaldehyde. These were prime attractions, often presented as the deformed offspring of crazed degenerate drug addicts. Authorites sometimes seized real punks, since possessing human remains is illegal in most jurisdictions. Fake punks, called "bouncers," are now more often exhibited, floating in jars of weak tea (the color hides the artificial look). Bouncers are also popular with showmen because they can be crafted with especially grotesque features.

Pit show—Show in which the attraction is displayed in a pit, like an alligator, snakes, sometimes a geek. The pit would generally not be an actual hole in the ground, but might be an area of the tent sectioned off by a low canvas divider, or a ground-level area viewed from above by the audience filing through on a raised walkway, or a wooden box serving as a cage open only at the top.

Pitch—To sell merchandise by lecturing and demonstrating, once common on carnival lots and city street corners, now almost exclusively found on late-night television infomercials (which would, in the old days, be called a "gadget pitch"). Many pitches included promises that valuable prize coupons would be found in certain boxes. Medicine pitches had a life of their own. Medicine pitchmen would travel rural areas, carrying entire crews of entertainers/salespeople, offering free entertainment and repeated opportunities to buy the sponsor's "medicine," usually a type of liniment.

Pitch cards—Cards containing photos and biographical information, sold for extra income by human oddities in a 10-in-1. Grace McDaniel, "The Mule-Faced Girl" was a famous human oddity, much in demand for her genuinely freakish appearance as well as her intelligence and professionalism. A "Fat Lady" on the *Strates Show* in 1941 said, "I know you folks in here would like to see me walking around. And while I'm walking around I have a few little souvenirs that I'll pass out to the men and the men only. Something you boys can have fun with, and you'll get more laughs out of than anything you've ever seen before. You can show them to the girlfriends or the wives, it's perfectly alright. Now as I said before, I pass them out to the men and the men only for ten cents each. If you'd like to have one now, I'm going to start on one end of the show and pass them around here just one time."

Punch and Judy—A traditional children's puppet show, unchanged in form and content for centuries, more familiar in its original form in Britain. The standard plot pits the shrill, violent Punch against his shrewish wife Judy, with an array of beatings and murder that would be wholly unacceptable to many modern adult sensibilities. In America, the term might refer to any puppet show, in ignorance of its origin. The show often appeared in old-time sideshows as entertainment for the children while their parents viewed stronger attractions. The "swazzle," the in-mouth whistle used to create the Punch puppet's voice, was sometimes sold as a pitch item.

Sideshow—Any show on the circus midway (since such a show would be ancillary to the "big show" (the circus.) However, the term can refer to carnival shows other than (for instance) "girl shows," and it most commonly refers to a freak show or 10-in-1. These days, sideshow also refers to the performance genre flowing from the old 10-in-1: from bed of nails and electric chair and sword-swallowing acts to piercing and geek acts.

Single-o—A show consisting of a single attraction, from railroad slang for "single occupancy."

Store show—In the off-season, especially during the Depression era, a good attraction might come into a town and rent an empty storefront to squeeze out some more performance time from the year. The best location was close to a Woolworth's five-and-dime store. The attraction would stay for a week in smaller towns, six weeks to two months (or as long as business would hold up) in larger towns.

Talker—*Never* barker. The man who makes the spiel to build a tip in front of an attraction. If he talks inside the attraction, he is a lecturer or inside talker.

Tip—The crowd gathered in front of an attraction to hear the outside talker's bally. They watch the free exhibition on the bally platform, and if the talker is convincing enough, he can "turn the tip," getting them to buy tickets and go in to see the show. When the entire tip has been turned by a talker's opening, it is said that he has "cleaned the midway."

Turn the tip—When the crowd of onlookers (the tip) watching a bally crowd up to the ticket box and start buying tickets, the talker has turned the tip. During the active ticket buying, he stops "spieling" (the selling portion of the bally) and "grinds," keeping up the excitement with rhythmic phrases (if a talker ever actually did say, "Hurry, hurry, hurry!" it would be during the grind.)

With it—"I'm with it" means "I work at this carnival (or at some other carnival)." Generally pronounced "widdit!" Some claim that it's not really used at all, favoring "on the show" as the actual term. A carnival term not used in the circus. If I was walking down a midway and an agent or a talker tried to call me in, I would say "With it." In other words, "You're wasting your breath talking to me."

Working act—A performer whose attraction is something he does (magician, contortionist, blockhead)—a skilled performer rather than just a human oddity.

PENN JILLETTE'S 10-IN-1 SCRIPT

PENN *is center stage in the dark.*

PENN

Everything Teller and I do in this show comes from a love that we share of the American side show, the freak show.

PENN *lights a candle, and he is seated on a stool center stage.*

PENN

Now the real name for the freak show is the Ten-in-One Show, and it's called the Ten-in-One Show because you get ten acts under one tent for one admission price. When I was a kid I used to go to the Franklin County Fair. That's where the carnival came near my hometown, and that fair would be in town about ten days every year, and every one of those ten days I'd go to the fair, and every day at the fair, I'd wind up at the Ten-in-One Show. And I loved the freak show. I loved it because you'd pay your 75 cents and you were allowed to go into a tent with people who were entirely different from you and then you could just stare at them. And I loved the freaks, but I especially loved the self-made freaks, the fire eater, the sword swallower, the tattooed people, because they had made an extra decision to be there, and I can remember standing in that tent watching that fire eater and I swear

©Reprinted with permission Penn Jillette

214

my whole life was there, it meant everything to me. And my friends would go with me to the Ten-in-One, but my friends were different, 'cause they took the whole show as some sort of weird challenge, and all through this fire eater's perfect act, my friends would be talking, and they'd be saying stuff like, "Oh, I know how he does that, Penn, he just coats his mouth with something." They would try to convince me there was some sort of something you could smear in your mouth, then go suck on a soldering iron, and it wasn't going to hurt you, right? And it's not just kids, it's also adults, and it's usually a man, and it's most often a man who's with some woman he's trying desperately, and often pathetically, to impress. And you'll hear this guy who just thinks he has to pretend to know everything, you know? So he's saying stuff like, "Oh, don't worry about him honey, he's just using cold fire." Or Needles. Now the reason that Teller and I are working together today, is that about fourteen years ago I saw Teller on stage in Jersey, alone and silently eating those needles. When I watched him up on that stage I got the same feeling in my guts that I used to get watching the fire eater as a kid, and I knew we had to work together, and we have been ever since. Now, I go in the lobby during intermission, I talk to folks and I hang out, I go outside. But the whole time I'm talking, I also try to listen, and I've learned a lot from eavesdropping on you guys for all these years. And one of the things I've learned is that there's a certain kind of person that comes to our show, and they may like the show, but they don't get it. And these are the people that cannot accept mystery. Now I want to try to make this clear to you, by people who can't accept mystery, I am not talking about scientists, and I am not talking about skeptics. 'Cause I'm a skeptic, and I've always felt that skeptics love the mystery, and that's why they don't want to believe in anything. They don't want to have any faith. They either want to have it scientifically proven over and over again, so it can't be denied and it works, or they want to leave it alone. That's it, they're okay with that. The kind of people that can't accept mystery are the kind of people that often seem the most mystical. They just believe the first thing they're told for their whole life, or they pretend to have an open mind, which means they believe anything they hear on Donahue. Or they'll make up something that makes sense to them and they'll just believe it. And it doesn't bother me that people are trying to figure out our stuff. It bothers me that they're wrong and they don't care. Just anything that will shut the mystery out of their heads and stop them from thinking. And I'll hear people doing this even with things as trivial as the Needles. I'll hear guys in the lobby with these real authoritative voices gathering little crowds of people going, "Oh, yeah, Needles, yeah, I figured that one out, sure, he's got a little pocket in the back of his throat, it's a skin graft from his leg, he just throws them right back in there." Or my favorite one, and I actually heard this, I did not make this up. Some stuff I just make up, but this I heard. There was a guy in L.A., who was talking about candy needles. Now I don't know where this guy ever heard of candy needles, but I assume he figured they're manufactured around Halloween time, as treats for the neighborhood children. I don't know. Anyways, about twenty years have passed, and those kids that I grew up with, I guess they're all still living in Greenfield, Massachusetts, and I turned out to be a fire eater, and the ironic thing I found out, is there's no trick. Not to this. To everything else in the show there's a trick, don't let anybody tell you differently. Susan floating in the air, she wasn't hypnotized, there's no balance point. If you want to try that at home, get a couple of chairs, clear your mind, study Yoga, you'll break your ass. It's a gimmick, it's a lie, it's a cheat, it's a swindle! But this is a stunt, and there's no such thing as cold fire. And if you still believe there is such a thing, and you think I'm be using it, wait 'til I get it lit, you raise your hand, I'll stick it in your eye, prove it to you.

TELLER *enters from stage left with the fire-eating props. Canister in left hand with thumb through removed top, one torch in canister. Second torch in right hand.*

PENN

Now Teller's coming out here with a fireproof camping fuel container. In it is lighter fluid, it's Ronson brand, and he's dipping the torches in.

TELLER *shifts torch in right hand to left hand held by middle finger against canister and removes torch that's soaking.* TELLER *exchanges the soaked torch with the dry torch (both are held in left hand momentarily), adjusts his grip on the soaked torch using his fingers that are holding the canister and hands* PENN *the soaked torch.* TELLER *takes the candle from* PENN.

PENN

The torches are cotton rope wrapped tightly around a metal rod that hooks into a wooden handle. It's not the cotton that burns, it's the fuel that burns and the way fire-eating works is this. You've got moisture throughout your mouth, and all that moisture has got to evaporate from any given part of your mouth, before that part will burn. So you learn how to handle the burning vapors, then you gotta make it look good. Now if you've got a lot of saliva in your mouth—and that's at least where I try to keep most of mine—you rub your lips right along the cotton and pull that vapor off.

TELLER *adjusts his grip on the candle so he can accept the torch from* PENN *using the last three fingers of his right hand. The torch is held under the candle by its handle.*

PENN

Now the vapor's still burning, but if you breathe in a little bit, the audience can't see it, so you got a beautiful surprise there. Then you just wait 'til the time is right and just let it flow, like it was magic smoke. When you want to put the fire out, there's a move for that, too, and it's the move that gives it the name "fire-eating." Now, you're not actually eating the flame, but I guess they figured that "oral fire-extinguishing" didn't sound that butch. When you feel your mouth drying out, you close your lips tightly, that cuts out most of the oxygen and *(snaps fingers)* the fire goes out.

PENN *hands torch to* TELLER.

PENN

Now when I was being taught this, I got burned every time I tried it.

PENN *takes candle from* TELLER. TELLER *redips torch that* PENN *just handed him by removing torch that was in canister and holding it in fingers of left hand alongside canister.*

PENN

And I still get burned occasionally, but the burns you get from fire-eating are for the most part extremely minor. They're the kind of burns you get—you know what I'm talking about—when you eat a pizza too fast, and that cheese is gonna snag you, or you gulp some hot coffee.

During the following, TELLER *exchanges the drying torch for the one soaking and prepares to hand it to* PENN.

PENN

Now I'm not trying to snow you no more. I'm not talking no mind over matter jive. There's no such thing, it just hurts like holy hell. But it's not dangerous. The dangerous thing is something lay people don't even think about, and that is every time you do this act, no matter how carefully or how well, you swallow about a teaspoon of the lighter fluid, and that stuff is poisonous. That's why they go to all that trouble to write "Harmful or Fatal If Swallowed" on every can, and the effect is, to a certain degree, cumulative. Now I say a certain degree. I do eight shows a week, I'm a big guy, that doesn't affect me. Carnies, the real boys, they'll do up to fifty shows a day, and in as little as two or three years that stuff'll build up in their liver and they'll get sick enough, they actually have to take time off and do another line of work in the carny while that liver regenerates, which, thankfully, it will do. Now I take the time to explain all of this to you in such detail because I think it's more fascinating to think of someone poisoning themselves to death slowly on stage than merely burning themselves, and after all, we're here to entertain you.

TELLER *hands torch to* PENN. PENN *hands candle to* TELLER.

PENN

I really tell you this 'cause this is the last bit in the show, and when you leave here tonight and you're thinking about our show, as I hope you will be, I don't want you to be thinking about how we did it. I want you to be thinking about why. So sit back and relax, I'm going to burn myself.

PENN *lights torch on candle in* TELLER'*s hand.* TELLER *has candle in right hand, canister with one torch soaking in left.*

PENN

This move right here and this move right here are called stalling. Now I realize you guys have been sitting in these seats a long time, but if you can just bear with us another moment, we'd like to look out at you guys. 'Cause there's an obvious but still unique quality of live theater, and that is that while we're doing the show, you're right here in the room with us. And that means we can see you. And if light happens to fall on one of your faces and we catch your eye, well, we'll look right in your eyes. And we'll do a small part of the show, couple lines, for you, and I mean, for you alone, you, staring right in your face, only you. And when we do that, and we've picked you, and you know it's you, 'cause you can just feel it, we're not paying any attention to you at all. We're trying to get the laughs, make the tricks work. We can't worry about you individually. So what I'm saying is that right now is the one place in the show that we're all in the same light and we can see you, and that's important. And I used to talk about the importance, but now I'm trying to learn to just shut up and look at you. Teller's got it down. And if you're the kind of person that needs to sum things up, all you need to know now is that you're in our tent, so it's okay, and the sideshow ain't dead. That's for damn sure.

TELLER *offers soaking torch in canister with left hand.* PENN *takes it.* TELLER *shifts candle to hand with canister.* PENN *puts out one torch and hands it over his head to* TELLER. TELLER *takes it with his right hand, dips it in the canister quickly and returns the torch to* PENN'*s waiting left hand.* PENN *does a few moves, and ends with both torches being put out.* PENN *then hands both torches to* TELLER'*s left hand (with canister in its).* TELLER *hands* PENN *the candle then redips both torches. When the torches are both dipped* TELLER *hold both in the fingers of his left hand (with the canister) and puts the canister top (held through it's ring top on* TELLER'*s left thumb since his entrance) on the canister.* TELLER *then places the canister on the deck behind* PENN. TELLER *is still holding the two dipped torches in his left hand.* PENN *has the candle. When* TELLER *stands from placing the canister, he shifts the torches in his left hand so he's able to hand them to* PENN *as one with handles toward* PENN.

PENN

No, no, no. Not yet, creeps. That was just the upper palate. I'd still like to burn my tongue. Now I realize this is a legitimate theater and you might not have been expecting this kind of hurricane hell driver jive out of us. And I just want to tell you if that half a knife blade that hooks over my middle finger with the load compartment that drips out the red paint, or Teller putting the needles in his mouth, or being underwater, or that last thing took you by surprise and uptightened you a little bit, this next thing will probably make you puke your guts out.

PENN *takes the dipped torches from* TELLER's *left hand.* TELLER *takes the candle with his left hand. His right hand is in his pants pocket. As* PENN *does a tongue transfer,* TELLER *removes cigarettes from his right pants pocket, puts one in his mouth and one in his right hand with filter toward* PENN *prepared to place it in* PENN's *mouth. Someone in the audience invariably moans.*

PENN

What the hell are you complaining about?

PENN *retains a flame in his mouth.* TELLER *lights a cigarette from the flame.* PENN *puts out the last torch.* TELLER *hands* PENN *a cigarette from his right hand.* PENN *lights it from the candle in* TELLER's *left hand.* PENN *and* TELLER *are just in candlelight.*

PENN

I've got a couple of announcements to make. First of all, I hope you all are hip enough to realize how many people it takes to put on a show like this, but there's a lot of people thanked in your program, and they all deserve it. Just to give you an idea, there are thirteen of us touring together on the road, led by C.B.—she's our stage manager—and that's just our crew. There's also house crew, house staff, management, publicity—it ain't no two-man show, that's for sure. I want to thank Richard, Tom, and Steve, our producers. And Marc Garland, who's my best buddy from high school, and Marc's been with us since way before the beginning. You don't even get to see him except for like a minute during Mofo, and the water tank, but he's really important. He handles all the props. He actually makes all the balloon animals, so at least he has something to fall back on. And he also stacks all our decks of cards, which is more important than you've hopefully realized. We're going to be here 'til [*insert day and date*] and we'd like some people in here, so if you liked the show at all and got an extra minute and could yap about it to your friends, we'd sure appreciate it. I notice there's quite a few kids here tonight. Kids, I don't want to insult you. I don't think you're stupid, but I've got to say this, so try to forgive me in advance, and that is to say the stuff we do here on stage is very dangerous, you shouldn't try any of it and you shouldn't even smoke cigarettes unless you want to look cool. My name is Penn Jillette. This is my partner, Teller. Thanks.

TELLER *blows out the candle.*

PENN *and* TELLER *stand and bow.*

They switch sides and bow again.

They exit up the aisles of the theater and out the front door, where they sell T-shirts, videos, records, hats, posters, etc.